Introduction to CATV

3rd Edition

Lawrence Harte

DiscoverNet
2474 Walnut Street, Suite 105
Cary, NC 27518 USA
Telephone: 1-919-301-0109
Fax: 1-919-557-2261
email: info@DiscoverNet.com
web: DiscoverNet.com

DiscoverNet
SOLUTION MARKETING

DiscoverNet

Printed and Bound by Lightning Source, TN.

International Standard Book Number: 9-781932813-18-0

About the Author

Lawrence Harte is senior editor of IPTV Magazine and Social TV Magazine where he has interviewed over 3800 companies since 2005. He is the founder of Internet TV Plus conferences and host of Internet TV Plus podcast. He is vice president of business development for roomioTV Hotel TV systems where he defined new services and installed/setup private television systems. Mr. Harte has worked for leading companies including Ericsson/General Electric, Audiovox/Toshiba and Westinghouse and has been an expert consultant for leading companies including Google TV, Samsung, Rovi, and others. As of 2017, he authored over 114 books on TV technologies and business on topics including Internet TV Systems, MPEG, and IPTV Basics. Mr. Harte holds many degrees and certificates including an Executive MBA from Wake Forest University (1995) and a BSET from the University of the State of New York, (1990).

Acknowledgements

Many smart people have helped to create this book. Some of them gave substantial amounts of time to share their experience, answer many questions, and invite us into their businesses and onto their production sets.

TV and Movie Production leaders and on air talent including Mike Davis from Uptone Pictures, Alisha Ramsey with AM Raleigh, George Wehmann from Raleigh Television Network, Scott Rucci with Rucci Productions, John Demers with Rusty Bucket kids TV show, Tim Bell from Blackett Bell Productions, John Draughon of iMedia Foundation, Tracie Clarke with WCAP News, Ross Cooper from Channel Islands, Drew Becker with Convey Media, and John Clark from ABC 11.

TV Technology and Business Professionals including Alex Terpstra with Civolution, Kirk Edwardson at Espial, Peter Maag from Haivision, Mark Reinhardt with Hargray, Toni Leiponen with Icareus, Mauro Bonomi from Minerva Networks, Rob Gelphman with MoCA Alliance, Rick Brown with NC State University, Chris Wagner from Neulion, Jonathan Witte with Ooyala, Tom Weiss from TV Genius, and Greg Fawson from XMediaResearch.

There have been many others who have shared their TV tech and business skills and experiences with me. Thank you all very much!

Table of Contents

Cable Television - CATV

Cable television (CATV) is a broadcast distribution system that uses a network of cables to deliver multiple types of media services. In the United States, companies (such as CATV) that provide programs over multiple transmission channels are called multichannel video programming distributors (MVPDs).

While CATV systems might use coaxial cables for a majority of customer connections, many CATV systems also use fiber optic cables and microwave transmission connections to transfer some of their signals.

Figure 1.1 shows a sample CATV system. This diagram shows that the CATV system gathers content from a variety of sources including network feeds, stored media, communication links and live studio sources. The head-end converts the media sources into a form that can be managed and dis-

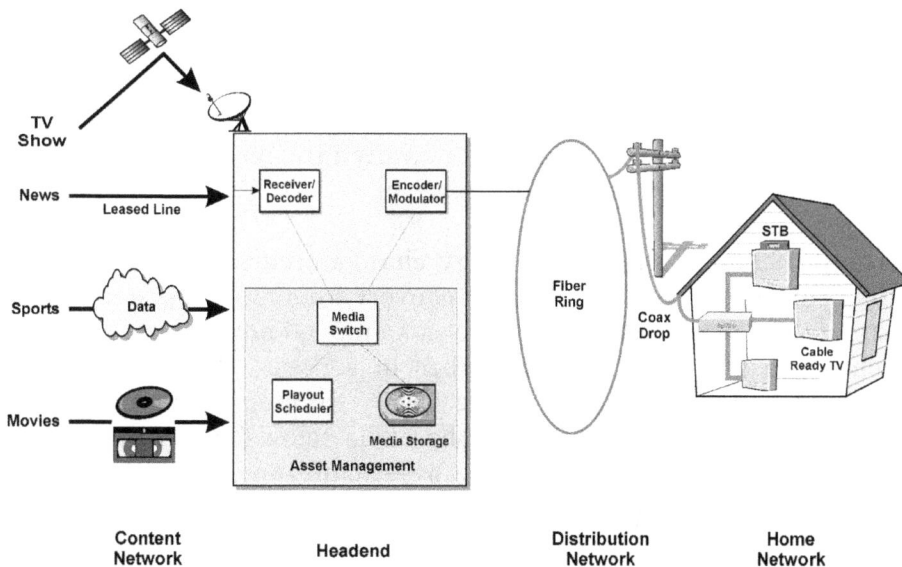

Figure 1.1, Cable Television – CATV System

tributed. The asset management system stores, moves and sends out (play-out) the media at scheduled times. The distribution system simultaneously transfers multiple channels to users who are connected to the CATV system. Users view CATV programming on televisions that are directly connected to the cable line (cable ready TVs) or through adapter boxes (set top boxes).

CATV systems were originally created to overcome some of the radio transmission challenges of early TV broadcast systems. In 1941, television broadcast services were providing news and entertainment to listeners by wireless broadcasting. Because television broadcast systems could only provide wireless coverage to a limited geographic area (such as a city), in 1948, people and companies began to be setup systems to deliver television signals in other areas by interconnection cables. These early analog cable television systems simply captured television signals in one geographic area by a receiving antenna and retransmitted these television channels in other geographic areas by a transmitting antenna.

For many years, wireless (television) broadcasters had significant control of the distribution of most forms of video media to the general public. This strong influence had resulted in strict regulations on the ownership, operation, and types of services broadcast companies could offer. For example, there are restrictions on the number and types of media systems (such as TV broadcast, cable TV, radio broadcast, and newspapers) can be owned by the same company within a geographic area. This is supposed to ensure that one company does not monopolize (and potentially influence or distort) the distribution of media within a specific area.

In the mid 1990's, a major technology change occurred in the broadcast industry. Television systems began to convert from analog systems to digital systems. The use of digital transmission enabled broadcasters to provide more channels and transmit new types of services. This included data (Internet) and telephone services. The ability to integrate several services into one transmission signal allows the cable television operator to offer these new services without significant investment in new cable systems.

Cable television systems were initially created because television broadcast signals could not reach some viewers. One of the first cable television systems occurred in remote valleys in Pennsylvania in 1948. Due to shadowing effects of mountains (signal blocking), people living in valleys solved their reception problems by installing antennas on top of the hills and running cables to their houses [1]. These early cable systems were simple antennas that used cable connections to retransmit signals to nearby areas.

As television signals travel through the cable distribution system, some of the signal energy is lost (signal attenuation) To overcome the signal attenuation losses of interconnection cables, amplifiers are inserted at regular intervals in cable systems to restore the original signal levels. Although amplifiers boost the signal levels, each amplifier adds signal distortion (electrical noise). Due to the cumulative effects of amplification noise, the use of amplifiers limits the maximum distance of a cable television distribution system. Amplifiers may be installed approximately every 1,000 feet [2].

In the 1950s, cable system operators began experimenting with the insertion of other television programs that were not available in their local areas. This allowed cable systems to offer programming that was unavailable via normal television broadcast. This increased the interest of customers in purchasing cable television services.

Each analog television channel uses 6 to 8 megahertz (MHz) of the radio spectrum to transfer both video signal (a majority of the bandwidth) and audio. In the United States, the Federal Communications Commission (FCC) initially allocated a frequency range within the very high frequency (VHF) radio spectrum (below 300 MHz) to allow the transmission of up to 12 television channels. To provide additional television channels, the FCC allocated additional frequencies in the ultrahigh frequency (UHF) portion of the radio spectrum (above 300 MHz). Channels 14 to 83 were created in the frequency range of 470 MHz to 894 MHz. The frequency bands for television channels 70 through 83 were eventually reallocated (reassigned) for mobile telephone services in the 1980s.

The first "pay-per-view" (PPV) channel was offered by a cable television system in Wilkes-Barre Pennsylvania in 1972 [2]. This was a regional service called home box office (HBO). In 1975, HBO began transmitting nationwide using satellite transmission. Early satellite systems could broadcast up to 24 channels for each satellite transponder. These early systems required the use of relatively large dish antennas 10 meters in diameter and each channel required a separate antenna. This limited the initial distribution of HBO to cable networks.

In 1976, cable systems began to use fiber optic cables to carry television signals from the head-end to the neighborhoods [3]. Some of the advantages of fiber-optic cable include lower signal losses than coaxial cable, higher data transmission rates and digital signal regeneration. The use of fiber optic cable reduced the need for amplifiers to be used between the head-end and customer from 30 to 40 down to approximately 1 or 2 [4].

Fiber optic cable has much more bandwidth transmission potential than coaxial cable. A typical coaxial cable system can transfer approximately 10 billion bits per second (Gbps). A single strand of fiber optic cable (and there are usually many fibers per cable) can carry in excess of 1 trillion bits of data (Tbps) [5]. When transferring information in digital form, the signal is regenerated at each amplifier rather than amplified.

Using multichannel digital video compression (MPEG), CATV systems can transmit several video channels (6 to 10) in the 6 MHz bandwidth of a single analog television channel [6]. When using the large available bandwidth of coax cable, more than 1,000 digital video channels can be provided to consumers.

Broadcast Television

Broadcast television is the wireless transmitting of video and audio signals to devices within a broadcast area (such as television sets) that can receive the broadcast signals. Television broadcast technology was initially developed in the 1940s. The success of the television marketplace is largely due to standardized, reliable, and relatively inexpensive television receivers and a large selection of media sources. The first television transmission standards used analog radio transmission to provide black and white video service. These initial television technologies have evolved to allow for both black and white and color television signals, along with advanced services such as stereo audio and closed caption text. The ability to enhance an existing system without changing the basic TV services was a very important evolution as it allowed new television services to be provided (such as color television) on the same radio channel as black and white television services.

Television systems initially used analog television technology. While analog television transmission provided relatively good video and audio signals, it does not easily allow the sending and receiving of multimedia signals and services. As a result, TV broadcast systems have been converted to use digital signal transmission. Each digital TV broadcast channel can provide several digital TV channels along with advanced television services.

New technologies allow transmission of high-definition television (HDTV). HDTV is the term used to describe a high-resolution video and high quality audio signal as compared to standard definition video transmission. HDTV signals can be in analog or digital form. Digital HDTV systems have the added benefits of providing data and other multimedia services.

To offer paid subscription services where only people who paid to watch these premium channels could see them, one-way cable TV systems used signal scrambling to protect premium channels. The premium channels would be modified at the head end with a scrambling code or process which required the viewer's equipment to use a code or process to descramble the signals. The TV broadcasters would provide customers who subscribed to the premium channels with equipment that could descramble the premium channels.

Figure 1.2 shows a television broadcast system. This television system consists of a television production studio, a high-power transmitter, a communications link between the studio and the transmitter, and network feeds for programming. The production studio controls and mixes the sources of information including videotapes, video studio, computer created images (such as captions), and other video sources. A high-power transmitter broadcasts a single television channel. The television studio is connected to the transmitter by a high bandwidth communications link that can pass video and control signals. This communications link may be a wired (coax) line or a microwave link. Many television stations receive their video source from a satellite television network. This allows a single video source to be relayed to many television transmitters.

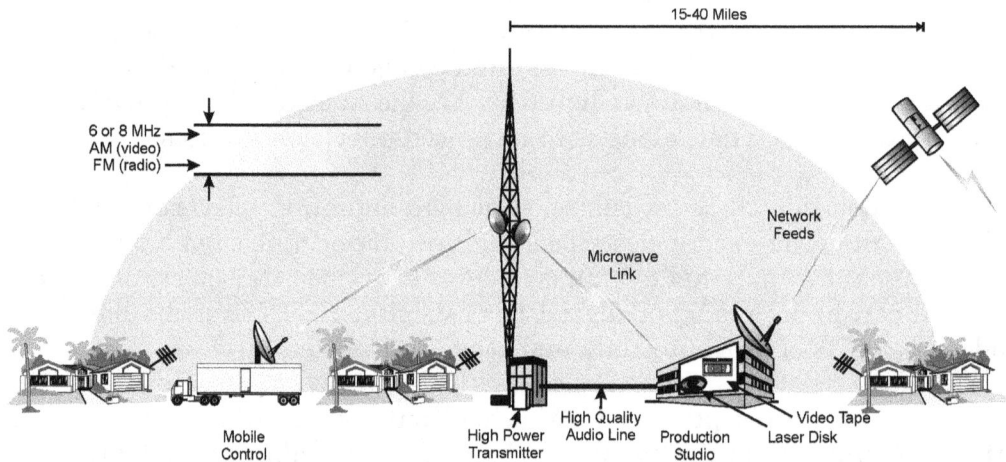

Figure 1.2, Broadcast Television System

One-Way Cable TV

One-way cable TV systems (only from the head-end to consumers) deliver programming content from one source to viewers that are connected to the system. Initially CATV systems were one way systems that captured broadcasted television programs ("off-air") and simply transferred these signals by cable for retransmission in another geographic area.

Initial CATV systems used a tree trunk distribution process. The broadcast signal of multiple channels is sent into the trunk of the tree and the signal is diverted to branches (neighborhoods) by tapping into the trunk. As the signal traveled through the branches of the tree, the level is reduced which required the use of amplifiers to boost the signal level up as it traveled further through the tree. To keep viewers from watching paid subscription services, the premium channels could be scrambled or blocking filters could be installed before the final connection reached the home keeping specific TV channels from entering into the home.

Figure 1.3 shows a one-way cable television system. This diagram shows that various video sources are selected in the head-end. Each of the video sources that will be distributed on the cable network is applied to an RF modulator that converts the video signals into RF signals on a specific frequency. The many RF signals are combined (added together), amplified and sent to the cable television system distribution network. The distribution network supplies part of the signal (signal tap) as the cable passes near each

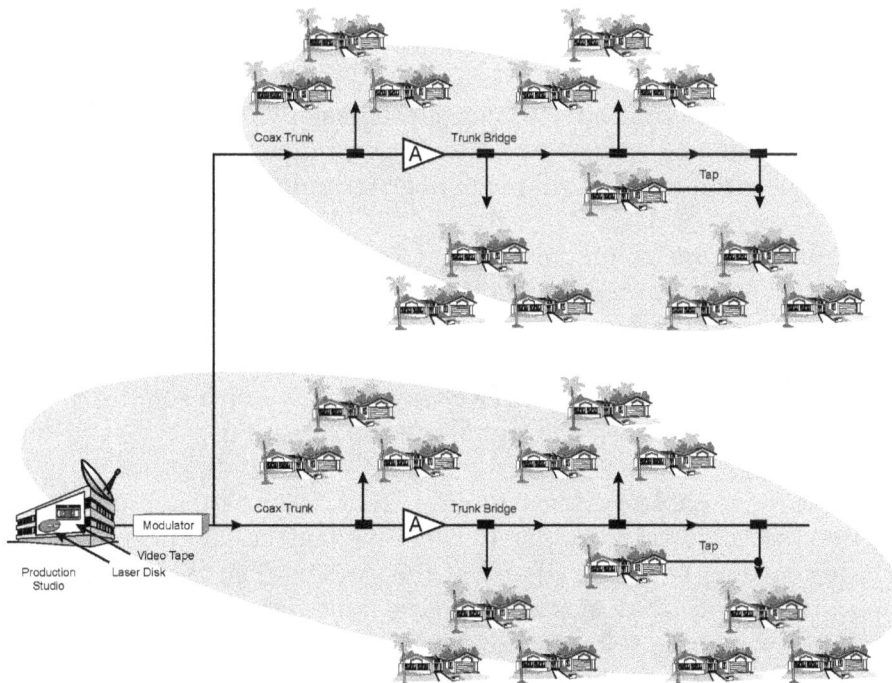

Figure 1.3, One-Way Cable Television System

home or business location. As the distribution system progresses away from the head-end, the signal level begins decrease. Periodically, amplifiers are used to increase the composite video signal.

Two-Way Cable TV

Two-way cable TV systems deliver programming content and receive commands and data from viewers that are connected to the system. Initially two-way CATV systems were hybrid systems (used separate networks) to send programming (cable trunk system) and receive responses (such as the telephone network). Cable TV systems have evolved to include forward and return channels on the same cable distribution system.

For two-way cable systems that use coaxial (RF) cable, return paths (return transmission channels) can be assigned to frequencies in the range below 50 MHz. This frequency range was unassigned for analog television operation because it was already assigned to other systems such as radio broadcasting. For cable systems that have converted their networks to use fiber (optical) cable, the systems can use separate fiber strands for each direction, as each fiber cable often has several (30+) fiber strands.

Two-way cable systems commonly convert some of their RF channels (usually upper frequency channels) to digital channels. Each digital cable channel transfers approximately 30 to 40 Mbps. This allows each digital cable channel to transport 6 to 10 digital TV channels (each digital TV channel only requires 2 to 4 Mbps of data). Two-way cable systems require bi-directional amplifiers which boost the signal in both directions.

To enable two-way cable systems to offer data services (such as Internet access), they use data transceivers (a cable modem) at the user end and a coordinating modem at the head-end of the system. The cable modem is a communication device that modulates and demodulates (MoDem) data signals to and from a cable television system. A modem at the head-end coordinates the customer's modem and interfaces data to other networks (such as the Internet).

Figure 1.4 shows a two-way cable television system. This diagram shows that the two-way cable television system adds a cable modem termination system (CMTS) at the head-end and a cable modem (CM) at the customer's location. The CMTS also provides an interface to other networks, such as the Internet.

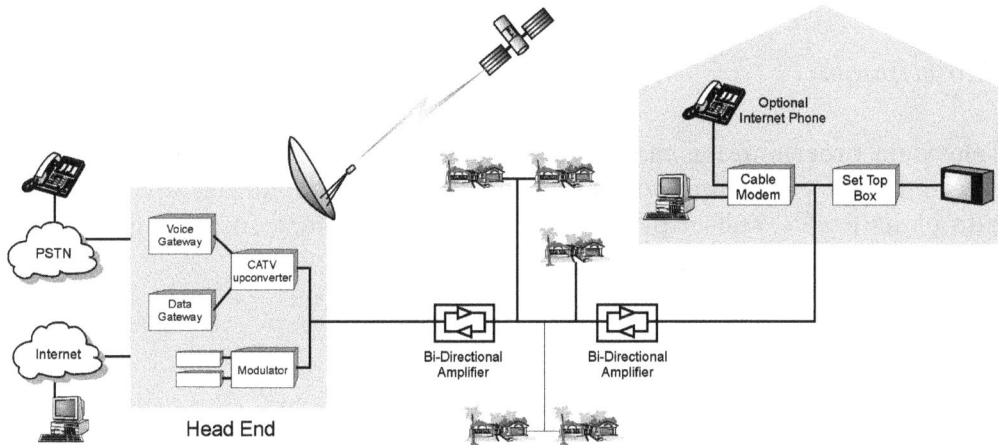

Figure 1.4, Two-Way Cable Television System

CATV Services

Services that are offered by cable television system operators include television programming, pay per view, advertising, data services (Internet access), telephone services, and television commerce (tcommerce).

Television Programming

Television programming involves the sending of television programs to groups of consumers that are connected to the cable television network. Television programs range from free programs (public service and advertiser paid) to premium programming (subscription paid and pay per view) services.

Free to Air

Free to air broadcasted media programs are transmissions that anyone can view if they have a receiver that can receive, process, and display the signal. Free to air may include promotional segments which are paid for by advertisers to help pay the costs of broadcasting the content.

Subscription

Television programming may also be provided on a subscription basis. To receive the programming, viewers must pay for the broadcast services. The rate plans for TV subscription services may be divided into group (tiered) rate plans.

Programming Tiers

Television service rate plans typically include at least three levels (tiers) of service. These include basic service, mid-level and premium services. The basic service rate plans typically include several local and regional television programs, such as news, weather, community and other relatively low cost programming. The mid-level service plans often add one or two groups of higher value channels, such as sports and some movie channels. Premium services typically include several groups of premium channels and 30 to 45 music channels. Some of the key rate plan differences include the individual pricing of channels, enhanced navigation options and an increase in the number of international channels.

Figure 1.5 shows sample cable TV rates throughout Asia, Europe and the USA. This table shows that the television service rates are often divided into basic, mid-level and premium groups and that the number of channels offered ranges from approximately 70 channels for basic service to over 160 channels for premium services.

Company	System Type	Basic	Mid-Level	Premium
Charter Communications, Allendale, MI-USA	Cable	$54.99 (76 chan + 1 groups)	$65.99 (76 chan + 2 groups)	$70.99 (76 chan + 1 group + all premium)
Cable TV - Hong Kong Hong Kong[2] (exchange rate used =.13)	Cable	$40.04 (63 chan)	$49.14 (70 chan)	$59.94 (76 chan)
NTL Cable-UK (exchange rate used = 1.89)	Cable	$7.04 (top 10 UK chan+)	$14.72 (100 chan)	$24.96 (160 chan)

Notes: 1. Cable TV Hong Kong rates calculated by adding 1 program group, other program groups were available

Figure 1.5, CATV Service Rate Comparison

Some of the fees associated with cable television service include an installation fee, equipment rental fees, deposits, monthly service fees and pay per view fees. The installation fee typically ranges from $30 to $150. There are various options for waiving (removing) the installation fee, ranging from having another service, special promotions or some other event that encourages the customer to take immediate action.

Equipment rental fees for the set top box range from $5 to $30 per month. According to the 18th FCC Report on Video Competition delivered to Congress in 2017, nearly all cable TV subscribers lease set top box equipment from their providers [7].

There is typically no rental fee charged for the broadband modem. Equipment deposits range from around $0 to $300. The amount of the deposit is affected by the length of the service contract (monthly, 1 year+). Pay per view fees range from around $1 to $5 per view. Special viewing events can be considerably higher than standard PPV charges.

Figure 1.6 shows a sample cable television service rate plan. This table shows that cable systems typically charge a setup fee of $30 to $150 and have equipment rental fees ranging from $5 to $30 per month. Some cable service providers do not require (waive) deposits and some do require deposits to ensure equipment is returned and not abused. Fees for TV monthly services range from $13 per month to more than $128 per month. Pay per view fees (PPV) typically cost $1 to $5 per view.

Fee	Cost
Installation	$30-$150
Equipment Rental	$5 to $30
Deposits	$0 to $300
Monthly Service Fees	$13 to $128
Pay per View (typical)	$1 to $5

Figure 1.6, TV Service Rate Samples

Pay per View (PPV)

Pay-per-view is a video signal subscription service that allows customers to pay for the individual video selections they desire to view. Pay-per-view service can be defined for specific events, time periods, or may be paid for (sponsored) by another company or person.

Pay Per Event

Pay per event is the authorization to obtain a program or access to a program on a definable set of conditions. An example of a pay per event is the authorization to watch a movie for a fee. The typical charge for pay per view services is approximately $6.00.

Pay Per Period

Pay per period is the authorization to obtain a program or access to a program over a defined time period. An example of a pay per period is the authorization to watch a movie or a group of movies for a fee where access to the content is authorized for a time period (such as 24 hours). A pay per time period may begin immediately, after the viewing of the program begins, or some other defined time period.

Sponsored Programs

Sponsored programs are media items (such as movies or games) that are provided to consumers or users where other people or companies pay for the cost of receiving or using the media. The payment may be a promotion incentive (a coupon for a free movies) or the payment may be authorized when a viewer provides their registration information (a sales lead).

TV Advertising

Advertising is the insertion or presentation of a promotional message or media content to one or more potential customers. The key types of cable television advertising include linear advertising (network advertising and local advertising) on demand advertising, enhanced advertising, and Interactive advertising.

Network advertising is advertising messages (adverts) are commonly provided by a TV network provider to local broadcasters in the affiliate distribution agreement. Local broadcasting companies (network affiliates) may receive television programs (network programs) at reduced or no cost in return for including network TV ads. TV networks provide some of the advertising time to be used by local broadcasters (typically 1 to 5 minutes per hour) which they can sell TV ads (to local businesses) in their local broadcasting area.

Linear Advertising

Linear advertising is the inserting of promotional messages into programs that are being transmitted in continuous form (broadcasting or streaming). Local advertising may be sold for $1 to $5 for each thousand viewers (cpm) for average viewership and higher rates $20 to $35 cpm may be charged for very popular movies and shows. Typical ad insert insertion rates are 6 to 12 spots (30 seconds each) per hour. Commercial may be grouped into longer time periods (called ad pods) such as 4 to 6 ads during a commercial break.

On Demand Advertising

On demand advertising is the inserting of promotional messages into programs that can be requested and flow controlled by the user. On demand advertising may be sold on a per view basis.

Enhanced Advertising

Enhanced advertising is the sending of modified content (personalized ads), additional media (offer messages), or data or signals along with the original advertising media that can enhance the ad viewing experience. Enhanced advertising may be addressed to specific viewers (addressable advertising) and may allow the viewer to see more targeted messages (offers that are specifically designated for the recipient or a group of recipients).

Dynamic Ad Insertion (DAI)

Dynamic ad insertion (DAI) is the process of inserting an advertising message into a media stream, such as a web page or television program, in which the ads can vary at different times or for different types of customers. DAI may by locally select from pre-stored ads or ads may be dynamically setup at the broadcasting source.

Replaced ads may be precisely targeted to the viewer dramatically increasing the advertising success rate and the fees the cable TV system operator can charge for advertising.

Interactive Advertising

Interactive advertising is the process of allowing a user to select or interact with an advertising message. Interactive advertising allows the advertiser to better target advertising messages and to receive direct feedback to the advertising message. Advertising fees for interactive advertising can be based on the type of interactive event. For example, when a viewer requests for additional product information on purchasing a car or house, a fee of $20 or more may be charged to the advertiser.

Company spending on advertising in all forms of media (television, radio, magazines, and Internet) increases each year with the gross national product (GNP). However, the percentage of advertising spent on traditional broadcast television shifting to digital media [8].

Data Services (Cable Modems)

Cable TV data service provides customers with the ability to transfer data through the cable TV system. This is usually in the form of Internet access but it can also include private data connections.

Cable TV Data Capacity

A single coax data line can provide up to 10 Gpbs of data service downstream and about 1 Gbps data service upstream (DOCSIS version 3.1.) Full DOCSIS 3.1 cable modem system released in 2016 can provide up to 10 Gbps of data transfer in either direction [9]. The data rate is shared by multiple homes that are connected to the same coax distribution system. Cable TV systems typically interconnect their coax access networks (hundreds of homes) using Giga or Terra bit fiber optic networks.

Internet Access

Customers usually pay a monthly fee for high-speed data connection in addition to an Internet service provider (ISP) account. Cable modem service rates can vary based on the type of use; business or residential, combined service discounts, data transfer rate and data transfer limits. Business service rates can be 2 to 10 times higher than residential service rates.

Cable modem service rates are commonly lower for customers who subscribe to other services (bundled) through the cable system (such as television or telephony services). Service plans start with a basic data transfer rate (e.g. 2 Mbps) and a premium fee may be charged to increase the data transfer rate. Most cable modem service plans offer unlimited amounts of data transfer.

The basic data transfer rates offered by cable TV companies are increasing as a result of competition from other broadband service providers such as DSL, optical systems, powerline data, and wireless broadband. While the data transfer limits of many cable systems are unlimited in 2017, this may change as a result of the increased use of broadband TV through the Internet service. Some users may transfer 10+ Gigabytes of data each day (about 2 GB for standard definition quality TV show transferred through the Internet). This can be 100 times higher than the average cable TV Internet data subscriber and the cable TV system may not be designed to provide such high data rates to many users.

Cable modem services commonly include the assignment of email addresses and an amount web storage area for web site hosting. Business packages commonly include higher data transfer rate options, along with an option to be assigned a static IP address (important for connecting web servers). Because business services may require that the cable company install and configure systems in areas that do not have established cable facilities (such as downtown commercial business areas), business services may require a 1 to 2 year service contract.

Leased Data Lines

Leased data lines are telecommunication lines or reserve data transmission capacity for the exclusive use of a single customer or company. Leased data lines often come with a guaranteed level of performance for connections between two points.

Figure 1.7 shows sample rate plans for high-speed cable modem data access. This chart shows that cable modem access cost varies if the service is for residential or business use. The residential service rate varies if it is included as part of a television service package or if it is used independent of other services. The business packages include basic and premium services where the premium service has higher data transmission rates and more web storage. The residential service plans do not require a service contract, while the business plans do require a service contract of 1 to 2 years in this example. This service rate plan does not charge the customer an activation fee if they

	Residential		Business	
	With TV Service	**Independent**	**Basic**	**Premium**
Monthly Access	$39.99	$49.99	$89.99	$179.99
Activation	$0	$50	$100	$0
Downlink Speed	2 Mbps	2 Mbps	2 Mbps	4 Mbps
Uplink Speed	256 kbps	256 kbps	256 kbps	512 kbps
Email Addresses	3	3	10	100
Web Storage	10 MB	10 MB	500 MB	2 GB
Static IP Address	N/A	N/A	$10	$10
Modem and Router Lease	$0	$0	$10	$10
Contract Length	None	None	1 Year	2 Years

Figure 1.7, Cable Modem Service Rates

are adding data service to their television rate plan. The business package allows the company to obtain a static (unchanging) IP address.

CATV Telephone Services

Cable TV system telephone services allow customers to originate and receive telephone calls through their cable connections. Cable telephone services commonly require the installation of a cable telephone adapter box at the home which adapts the standard telephone signals to data signals that can be transferred on the cable TV system. Some cable TV companies have the capability to transfer (port) the customer's existing telephone to the cable TV system.

Telephone Services

Cable telephone service rates can vary based on the type of use (business or residential), combined service discounts, calling rate plans and call processing features. Business service rates (if available) can be several times higher than residential service rates. Cable telephone service rates can be lower for customers who subscribe to other services (bundled) through the cable system (such as data modem services).

Cable telephone calling rate plans start with a basic service rate (a telephone line) and additional premium calling rate plans may be added to the basic plan. Some cable telephone service plans offer unlimited domestic long distance calling and discounted international calling rates.

In general, cable telephone service rate costs have been decreasing due to competition from other telephone service providers, such as Internet telephone and mobile telephone providers.

Telephone Features

Cable telephone service plans commonly include a bundle of call processing services, such as call waiting, caller identification and call transfer. Some cable TV systems charge a premium for advanced call processing features, such as voice mail.

Telephone Number Portability

Telephone number portability in cable TV systems involves the ability for a telephone number to be transferred between different types of service providers. This allows customers to change service providers (such as from a telephone company to a cable TV provider) without having to change telephone numbers. Number portability also requires that the cable TV company transfer the telephone number to other types of operators (such as mobile telephone companies) and there is a cost to managing transferred telephone numbers.

Figure 1.8 shows a sample rate plan for cable telephone service. This chart shows that cable telephone access cost varies if the service is for residential

	Residential		Business	
	With TV Service	Independent	Basic	Premium
Monthly Access	$24.99	$34.99	$49.99	$79.99
Activation	$0	$50	$100	$0
Domestic Long Distance	$0	5 cents/min	5 cents/min	$0
International Long Distance	Varies by Country	Varies by Country	Varies by Country	5 cents/min certain countries
Call Features	Included	Included	Included	Included
Voice Mail	$3	$3	$10	$0

Figure 1.8, CATV Telephone Rate Plans

or business use. The residential service rate varies if it is included as part of a television service package or if it is used independent of other services. The business packages include basic and premium services. The premium service offers lower costs on domestic and international calls.

Television Commerce (Tcommerce) Service

Television commerce is a shopping medium that uses a television network to present products (video catalog), process orders, and receive payments. Examples of tcommerce include shopping channel shared revenue and sales revenue spits with paid programs (infomercials.)

Video Catalog

A video catalog is the presenting of items available for selecting or ordering in a video format. Video catalog formats can range from a linear progression of products (such as a television shopping channel) to an interactive video shopping cart that allows users to search and find items. Cable TV systems may charge fees to setup a video catalog and to list products within the catalog.

Order Processing

Order processing are the steps involved in selecting the products and agreeing to the terms that are required for a person or company to obtain products or services. Cable TV systems may receive transaction fees for processing orders and the transaction fees may be a combination of a per-order service (such as 50 cents per order) charge combined with a percentage the sale (such as 10% of sales).

Payment Processing

Payment processing is the tasks and functions that are used to collect payments from the buyer of products and services. Payments may be collected directly by the advertiser (using their merchant processor) or it may be performed by the TV broadcaster. The TV broadcaster may allow order to be paid via the television bill. When the TV broadcaster collects the money (this increases the risk of non-payment to the TV broadcaster), an additional payment processing fee may be charged.

Smart TVs and connected devices can use software programs (TV Apps) to display promotional offers and process sales using Internet connections. This allows cable TV providers and viewing device providers (such as Bluray Players) to add tcommerce services without significant (or any) changes to Cable TV systems.

Figure 1.9 shows how a vendor may receive a television commerce (tcommerce) order report. This example shows that a tcommerce vendor may receive payment from a tcommerce customer directly by cash or a credit card transaction, the customer may be able to place the order on their television bill or the customer may use a 3rd party such as Paypal to pay for the transaction.

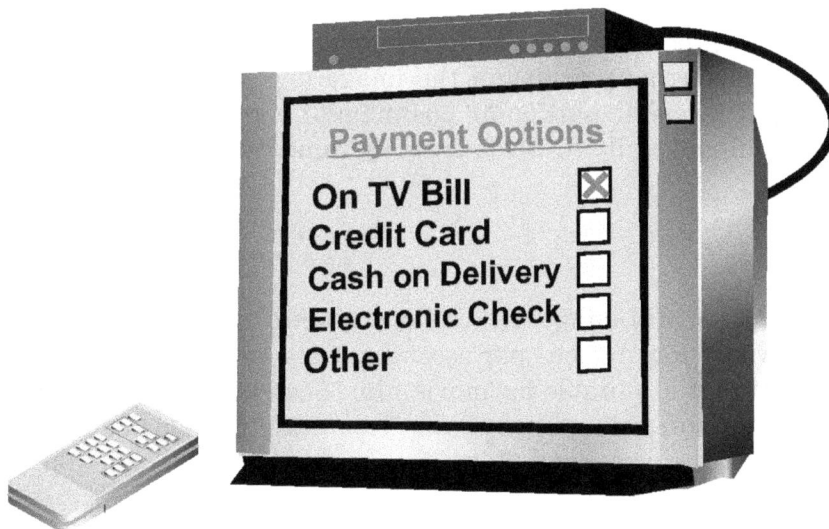

Figure 1.9, Television Commerce (Tcommerce)

Technologies

Some of the key technologies used in CATV systems include analog video, digital video, cable modem, high definition television (HDTV), 3DTV, cable telephony, wireless cable, interactive TV, TV Apps, IPTV, OTT, and Social TV.

Analog Video

Analog video contains a rapidly changing signal (analog) that represents the luminance and color information of a video picture. Sending a video picture involves the creation and transfer of a sequence of individual still pictures called frames. Each frame is divided into horizontal and vertical lines. To create a single frame picture on a television set, the frame is drawn line by line.

Scan Lines

Scanning is the process of converting an image into information signals by sequentially converting portions of the image (e.g. lines) into signals that represent light levels at particular positions of the image. For analog TV systems, scanning usually involves creating hundreds of lines per image.

Frames

A frame is a single still image within the sequence of images that comprise the video. Twenty four frames per second (24 fps) are considered the slowest frame rate that is suitable for movie film. Because television uses interlacing (frames of interspaced lines), the frame rate for television signals is typically 50 fps for Europe and 60 fps for the Americas.

Interleaving

The frames are drawn on analog systems to the screen in two separate scans. The first scan draws half of the picture and the second scan draws between the lines of the first scan. This alternating scanning method is called interlacing. Each field (interlaced frame) contains half of the video scan lines that make up the picture; the first field typically containing the odd numbered scan lines and the second field typically containing the even numbered scan lines. The use of interleaving reduces the amount of bandwidth required to transfer the television signal.

There are three primary systems used for analog television broadcasting: NTSC, PAL, and SECAM. The National Television System Committee (NTSC) is used for the Americas, while PAL and SECAM are primarily used in the UK and other countries. The major difference between the analog television systems is the number of lines of resolution and the methods used for color transmission.

There have been enhancements made to analog video systems over the past 50 years. These include color video, stereo audio, separate audio programming channels, slow data rate digital transfer (for closed captioning) and ghost canceling. The next major change to television technology will be its conversion to HDTV.

Figure 1.10 demonstrates the operation of the basic analog television system. The video source is broken into 30 frames per second and is converted into multiple lines per frame. Each video line transmission begins with a burst pulse (called a sync pulse) that is followed by a signal that represents color and intensity. The time relative to the starting sync is the position on the line from left to right. Each line is sent until a frame is complete and the next frame can begin. The television receiver decodes the video signal to position and control the intensity of an electronic beam that scans the phosphorus tube ("picture tube") to recreate the display.

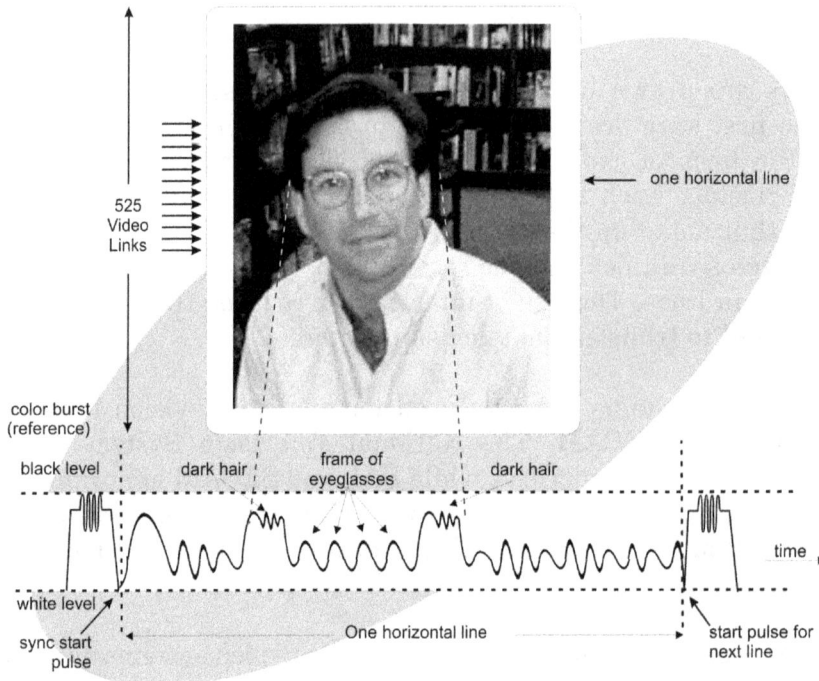

Figure 1.10, Analog Video

Digital Video

Digital video is a sequence of picture signals (frames) that are represented by binary data (bits) that describe a finite set of color and luminance levels. Sending a digital video picture involves the conversion of a image (such as NTSC or PAL format) into digital information that is transferred to a digital video receiver. The digital information contains characteristics of the video signal and the position of the image (bit location) that will be displayed.

The uncompressed digital video form is then sequenced (structured) for transmission in serial form. Serial digital video formats include serial digital interface (SDI) and asynchronous digital interface (ASI) formats.

Video Digitization

Sending a digital video picture involves the conversion of a scanned image to digital information that is transferred to a digital video receiver. The digital information contains characteristics of the video signal and the position of the image (bit location) that will be displayed.

Figure 1.11 shows a basic process that may be used to digitize images for pictures and video. For color images, each line of image is divided (filtered) into its color components (red, green and blue components). Each position on filtered image is scanned or sampled and converted to a level. Each sampled level is converted into a digital signal.

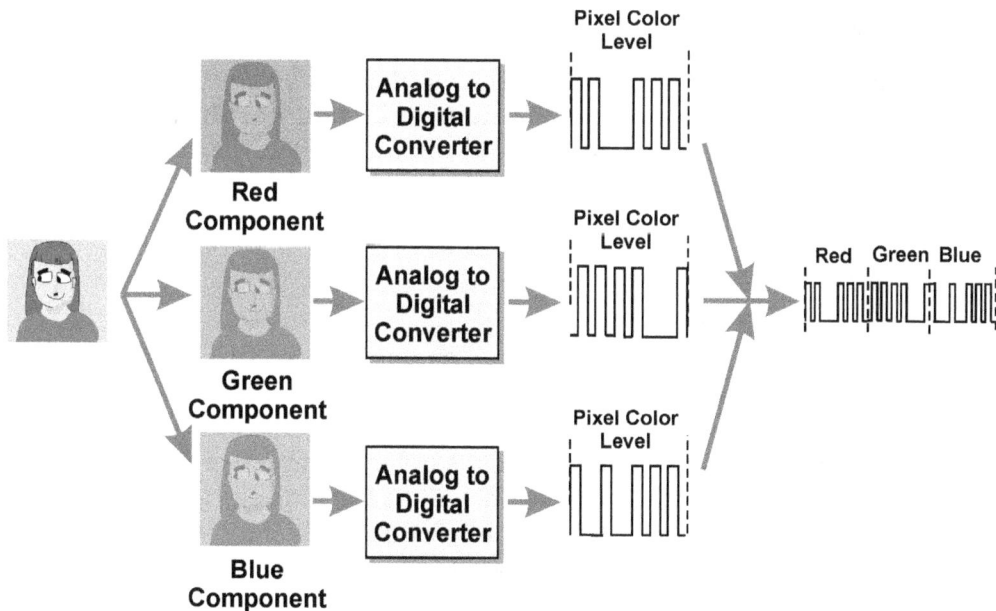

Figure 1.11, Video Digitization

Digital Video Compression

Digital video signals require a large amount of transmission bandwidth - 270 Mbps for standard definition and 1.5 Gps for HD. Higher data rates are needed for other uncompressed formats such as UIID (4k) and 3D.

To reduce the transmission bandwidth (an increase the number of channels that can be broadcasted), the information in digital video is compressed within frames (spatial compression) and between frames (time compression). Because compressed digital video requires a smaller amount of bandwidth (2 Mbps to 4 Mbps) than is available on a single digital transmission channel (30 Mbps to 40 Mbps), multiple digital TV programs can be sent on one transmission channel (simulcasting).

Frame Compression (Spatial)

Each separate image in a video sequence can be analyzed and compressed into component parts. For example, if the picture was a view of the blue sky, this could be characterized by a small number of data bits that indicate the color (blue) and the starting corner and ending corner. This may require much less bits than sending the bits that represent each pixel.

Time Compression (Temporal)

In addition to the data compression used on one picture (one frame), digital compression allows the comparison between frames. This allows the repeating of sections of a previous frame. For example, a single frame may be a picture of a city with many buildings. This is a very complex picture and data compression will not be able to be as efficient as the blue sky example above. However, the next frame will be another picture of the city with only a few changes. The data compression can send only the data that has changed between frames.

Simulcasting

Digital television broadcasting that uses video compression technology allows for "simulcasting" (simultaneously sending) several "standard definition" television channels (normally four to ten channels) in the same bandwidth as one standard analog television channel. The additional digital channels can be used for video or other types of digital services such as program downloads or music channels. Unfortunately, high definition digital television channels require a much higher data transmission rate and it is likely that only one or two HDTV channels can be sent on each digital RF transmission channel.

Figure 1.12 demonstrates the operation of the basic digital video compression system. Each video frame is digitized and then sent for digital compression. The digital compression process creates a sequence of frames (images) that start with a key frame. The key frame is digitized and used as

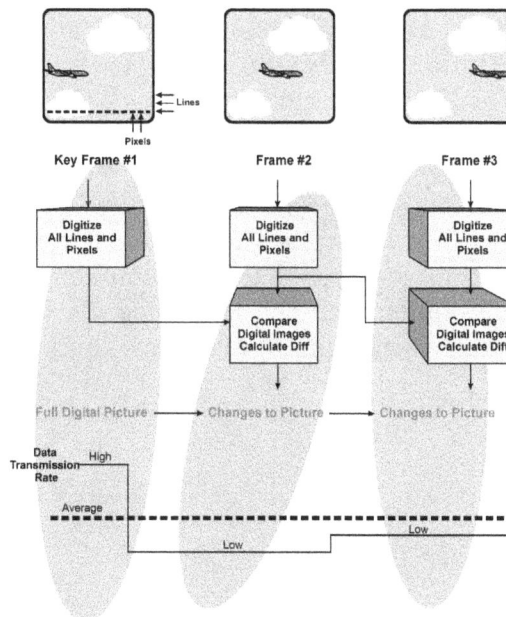

Figure 1.12, Digital Video

reference points for the compression process. Between the key frames, only the differences in images are transmitted. This dramatically reduces the data transmission rate to represent a digital video signal, as an uncompressed digital video signal requires over 270 Mbps compared to less than 4 Mbps for a typical digital video disk (DVD) digital video signal.

Digital Video Interconnection Types

There are several digital video connection types that enable broadcast quality video and audio equipment to interconnect with each other. Some of the key interconnection types include HDMI, SDI, ASI, and IP Video.

High Definition Multimedia Interface (HDMI)

High Definition Multimedia Interface (HDMI) is a short distance (typically up to 50 feet) interconnection specification which combines a digital video interface (DVI) connection, along with the security protocol HDCP. HDMI has the ability to determine if security processes are available on the DVI connection and, if not, the HDMI interface will reduce the quality (lower resolution) of the digital video signal.

HDMI was primarily developed for consumer electronics devices. While it can be used for transfer of uncompressed professional video signals (called Clean HDMI), it lacks certain features that are helpful for professional video equipment such as time stamps and the HDCP security requirement can cause difficulty when using professional production equipment.

Figure 1.13 shows the evolution of HDMI capabilities. The origin HDMI 1.0 transferred up to 4 Gbps and could provide up to 8 audio channels. HDMI 1.1 added DVD audio capability. HDMA 1.2 included super audio CDs and new CEC controls. HDMI 1.3 could transfer up to 10 Gbps, added more color modes, additional CEC control capabilities, defined certification testing, and added a mini connector type. HDMI 1.4 added 4k theater resolution, 100 Mbps Ethernet, audio return channel, 3D, and added a micro connector type. HDMI 2.0 can transfer up to 18 Gbps, has more CEC controls, and supports HDR video. HDMI 2.1 (*planned) can transfer up to 48 Gbps, up to 10k resolution, has game mode, and can transfer dynamic HDR video.

HDMI Version	Year	Capabilities
HDMI 1.0	2002	Up to 4 Gbps - 8 channel audio
HDMI 1.1	2004	added DVD Audio
HDMI 1.2	2005	added Super Audio CDs, sRGB capability, CEC control capabilities
HDMI 1.3	2006	up to 10 Gbps, new color mode capabilities, more CEC controls, testing, and mini connector
HDMI 1.4	2009	added 4K theater resolution, 100 Mbps shared Ethernet, audio return channel (ARC), 3D, Micro HDMI
HDMI 2.0	2013	up to 18 Gbps (6 Gbps per channel), HDR video, more CEC controls
HDMI 2.1 (*planned)	2017	up to 48 Gbps, up to 10k resolution, game mode, added dynamic HDR, higher resolutions

Figure 1.13, HDMI Versions

Serial Digital Interface (SDI)

Serial digital interface (SDI) is high-speed coax professional digital media transmission system developed by the Society of Motion Picture and Television Engineers (SMPTE) which allows multiple media sources to be time synchronized with each other. SDI can send multiple uncompressed digital video and audio along with control information and typically up to 300 feet.. The specification has evolved over time to allow the transfer of higher-resolution media (SD, HD, UHD), audio (multichannels) and advanced features (3D).

SDI uses the format that allows the addressing and transmission of professional digital media files between digital media devices such as camcorders, DVRs and editing systems. SDTI is a media format that is compatible with and builds on the SDI interface. SDI has evolved to provide multiple data rates including 270 Mbps (SD-SDI), 1.485 Gbps (HD-SDI), and 2.970 Gbps (3G-SDI). SDI continues to evolve as new digital media formats become available. A fiber optic version of SDI is available which can be used for long-distance connections.

Figure 1.14 shows that serial digital interface (SDI) connections have evolved from standard definition (270 Mbps, 360 Mbps) connections up to 24 Gbps.

Version	Year	Key Features
SD-SDI	1989	Up to 360 Mbps
ED-SDI		Up to 540 Mbps
HD-SDI	1998	Up to 1.485 Gbps
Dual Link HD-SDI	2002	Up to 2.970 Gbps
3G-SDI	2006	Up to 2.970 Gbps
6G-SDI	2015	Up to 6 Gbps
12G-SDI	2015	Up to 12 Gbps
24G-SDI		Up to 24 Gbps

Figure 1.14, SDI Versions

Asynchronous Serial Interface (ASI)

Asynchronous serial interface is a serial transmission format standard that is used to transport MPEG-TS (multi-channel) compressed digital video signals. ASI is used as the feed for the final broadcast signal that is sent to the coaxial, optical, or wireless broadcast systems.

Internet Protocol Video (IP Video)

TV production and broadcasting equipment is transitioning from highly structured synchronized connections (SDI) to more flexible packet data systems (Internet Protocol - IP.) IP Video uses standard Internet protocols to setup and manage transmission and control connections between devices and networks. The data connections may use standard common off-the-shelf (COTS) network equipment and systems.

To select which standard protocols to use (there are many to choose from), the alliance for IP Media solutions organization has been setup (aimsalliance.org.) The AIMS alliance is composed of many equipment and service companies working together to create an open system that allows devices to easily connect with each other and discover their capabilities.

Content Protection

Content Protection is the processes that are used to prevent media or programs (content) from being pirated or tampered with in a communication network (such as in a television system.) Content protection involves uniquely identifying content, assigning the usage rights, scrambling and encrypting the digital assets prior to play-out or storage (both in the network or end user devices) and delivering the accompanying rights to allow legal users to access the content.

Physical Access

Physical access is the ability of a user or unauthorized user to physically send or receive information with a communication system or device. By restricting access to cable TV lines, the cable TV operator can prevent unauthorized access (of its signals). Some cable TV systems use locking RF connectors that required a special tool or key to allow the connecter to be installed or removed. Because it is relatively easy to overcome the restrictions of physical access, cable TV system operators have been shifting to protecting content using electronic processes.

Service Authorization

Service authorization is the process of validating a subscriber or device to request or obtain services. Cable TV companies perform service authorization by installing conditional access systems. Conditional access systems can use uniquely identifiable devices (sealed with serial numbers) and may use smart cards to store and access secret codes that are used to validate the identity (authentication) and control access (authorization) to services (content).

Video Scrambling

To protect premium (non-free) content from being viewed by unauthorized people (unpaid), cable TV operators can modify (scramble) the video signals of premium channels. Video signal scrambling changes the electrical signal (often distortion of video, digital voice, or data) to prevent interpretation of the signals by unauthorized users that are able to receive the signal. Because the scrambling process is performed according to a known procedure or algorithm, the received signal can be descrambled to recover the original digital stream through the use of a known code or filtering technique.

In 1971, the first system to use scrambling on a cable system was demonstrated [10]. The first scrambling suppressed the synchronization signal so the video of the television picture was distorted. To decode the scrambled video, the synchronization signal was recreated in the setup box by decoding the correct synchronization signal from another portion of the transmitted signal. Another form of signal scrambling that was used was the insertion of a signal that was slightly offset from the channel's frequency to interfere with the picture.

These early video signal scrambling systems were relatively simple in design. As a result, accessory devices soon became available that allowed consumers to decode the scrambled signals without paying subscription fees. To prevent unauthorized viewing, more sophisticated signal scrambling technologies have been developed and the upgrading of cable TV systems to digital transmission has enabled more sophisticated encryption processes.

Encryption

For digital television signals, digital video signals can be easily modified (encrypted) with using codes (keys) and modification processes (algorithms). To successfully decode the video signal, the set-top box must contain decryption key code(s) and algorithm(s). For two-way cable systems, the codes and encryption algorithms can be dynamically and decoding data continuously changed and unauthorized viewing has been greatly reduced.

Watermarking

Watermarking is a process of adding or changing information in an analog or digital video media tape, streaming media or other form of video media to uniquely identify the media and/or its authorized uses. Video watermarking may be performed by adding or slightly modifying the colors and/or light intensities in the video in such a way that the viewer does not notice the watermarking information.

Watermarking can be performed on a broadcast channel or on individual streaming channels. Watermarking information may include the source, distribution channel, authorization codes, date and time stamps, and other types of information.

Watermarking can be used to enable the discovery of the source and distribution of unauthorized uses of content (digital forensics.)

Cable Modem Technology

Cable modem technology involves the reception and conversion of digital information into RF channels that can be transferred on the cable TV system. Digital RF channels are structured to allow the transferring of data packets to and from specific cable modems. Cable modems transfer data from users to the system using shared access transmission. Cable modem systems are increasing their data transmission rates by combining (bonding) multiple RF channels together.

Digital RF Channels

To provide cable modem data services, some of the RF channels in cable TV system use digital modulation and frame structures which can be used to transport data (system control and user data.) Digital RF channels on cable TV system can transport approximately 30 Mbps to 40 Mbps. Some cable systems simulcast 120 RF channels providing a gross data transmission rate on a signal line of over 4 Gbps (30 Mbps x 120 RF Channels.) DOCSIS 3.1 includes a new modulation option which can increase the maximum data transmission rate to 10 Gbps.

Shared Uplink Access

Data that is transmitted on the downlink channel (from the headend) can be coordinated and scheduled each user. Data that is transmitting from the users on the uplink is random and must shared access to uplink RF channels. Because of the added complexity of sharing uplink channels, the capacity of the uplink channels (2 Mbps to 10 Mbps) is generally much lower than the downlink channels (30 Mbps to 40 Mbps). The DOCSIS 3.1 system can have uplink data transmission rates up to 1 Gbps.

Channel Bonding

Channel bonding is the grouping of RF transmission channels for a single service. Newer versions of cable modem systems can combine RF channels in either direction, providing for user data transmission rates of over 300 Mbps.

Figure 1.15 shows a block diagram of a typical cable modem system. This diagram shows that the Internet is connected to the head-end of the cable system by a gateway. The gateway adapts the data to and from the Internet

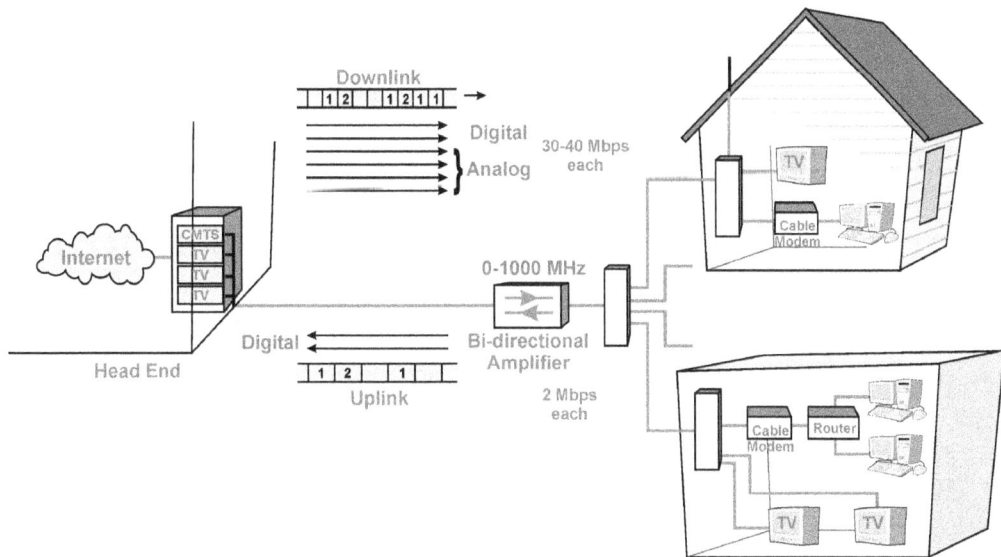

Figure 1.15, Cable Modem System

into a form that can be transmitted through the cable modem system. The cable modems at the head-end convert the digital signals into RF signals that can be transmitted through the cable network. A single 6 MHz (North America) or 8 MHz (Europe) RF television channel is converted to a high-speed data channel (30-40 Mbps) that is transmitted to all the users in the cable modem network. To access data on this channel, each cable modem is assigned a portion of the data channel from the CMTS at the head-end. This diagram shows that multiple RF channels may be used to provide more data transfer capabilities to each customer. When the cable modem at the customer's location wants to send data, it randomly accesses the system through a return RF channel.

High Definition Television (HDTV)

High definition television (HDTV) is a TV broadcast system that provides higher picture resolution (detail and fidelity) than is provided by conventional analog (e.g. NTSC or PAL) television signals. HDTV signals can be in analog or digital form and can have multiple resolution formats (1k HD, 4k UHD.)

High Resolution Video

HDTV has been offered in several countries since its introduction in Japan in 1988 [11]. The first HDTV receivers in the United States were introduced at the 1998 Winter Consumer Electronics Show in Las Vegas.

HDTV radio broadcast channels can use the same 6 MHz channel bandwidth. However, the existing NTSC signal must be replaced with a new high resolution analog or high speed digital radio signal. Initial demonstrations of HDTV required 2 standard television channels. The FCC has finally approved the "Grand Alliance" standard for high-definition television for the United States that only requires one standard television channel to send a HDTV digital channel and supplementary services.

Analog HDTV

Analog HDTV is the providing of television signals in high-resolution form using analog transmission. While it is possible to provide HDTV signals in analog formats, most HD transmission are provided in digital formats.

Digital HDTV

Digital HDTV is the transmission of video signals that have at least 2 times the number of lines (vertical resolution) and twice the number of pixels per line (horizontal resolution). HD results in a data transmission rates that are approximately 4 times higher than standard definition video. The data transmission rate of the HDTV system is 19 Mbps for MPEG-2 video compression and approximately 6-8 Mbps fro MPEG-4 AVC (part 10) compression format.

The specifications for HDTV digital systems allow for many types of data services in addition to digital video service. Digital HDTV channels carry high-speed digital services that can be addressed to a specific customer or group of customers that are capable of decoding and using those services. Examples of these services include: special programming information, software delivery, video or audio delivery (like pay-per-view programming), and instructional materials. The data rate available for additional services is dynamic and ranges from a few kbps to several Mbps, depending on the mix of video and audio program content.

Figure 1.16 shows comparison of MPEG-2 and the new MPEG-4/AVC video coding system. This diagram shows that the standard MPEG-2 video com-

	MPEG-2	MPEG-4/AVC or VC-1
Standard Definition (SD)	3.8 Mbps	1.8 Mbps
High Definition (HD)	19 Mbps	6-8 Mbps

Figure 1.16, High Definition Television

pression system requires approximately 3.8 Mbps for standard definition (SD) television and 19 Mbps for high definition (HD) television. The MPEG-4 AVC video coding system requires approximately 1.8 Mbps for SD television and 6 to 8 Mbps for HD television.

Ultra High-Definition (UHD)

Ultra High Definition (UHD) is a version of HDTV that has a minimum resolution of 3840×2160 pixels - commonly called 4K HD.

3 Dimensional Television (3DTV)

Three dimensional television (3DTV) is the providing of video signals that allows viewers to receive content that contains depth information (size, shadowing, and image differences between the left and right eyes). Depth perception can be created by using a variety of visual processes including 3D viewpoints (stereoscopic vision), multiple viewpoints (multiview), or full depth image creation (holographic).

Stereoscopic 3DTV (S3D)

Stereoscopic 3D is the process of adding depth perception to an image or video by using two viewpoint channels looking at a single point (object). The amount of image difference between the left and right eyes can be approximately 10% (limited amount of bandwidth needed to create 3D views).

Autostereoscopic

Autostereoscopic is the ability to directly provide dual-channel visual perception without the use of accessories such as filtering glasses. To create depth images without glasses, the display device must project separate images (stereoscopic) that can be seen separately by the right and left eyes. This may be accomplished by the use of tiny lenses on the projector (e.g. TV screen) that redirect image elements (pixels) dependent on the viewing position (specific locations where the viewer may sit or stand). When the viewer moves, they images they see come from different pixels.

Multi-Viewpoint 3DTV (M3D)

Multiview 3D is the process of adding depth perception to an image or video by using three or more viewpoint channels (can be 50+). Having multiple viewpoints allows the display to present depth at different viewpoints. Because each viewpoint tends to have unique image formats, the amount of data needed for each viewpoint is high.

3D television displays can use tiny multiple lens technology (Lenticular) to create multiple image beams (left and right) that allows a person to see depth without the need for glasses. Each of the cylindrical lenticules focus pixel images below it to a particular focal point. By installing a display with multiple lenticular lenses, as the viewer moves to different viewing points, they can see different pixels below the lenticules.

Figure 1.17 shows how a multiview lenticular display can provide depth perception and allow multiple viewers to have different perspectives. This example shows that the display provides several viewpoints that display different left and right images. Each of the viewpoints sees different pixels located behind the lenticular lens. As the viewer moves to different points, they can see different display pairs. This allows the viewer to have a different image with depth perception at multiple locations in front of the display without the need for eyewear accessories.

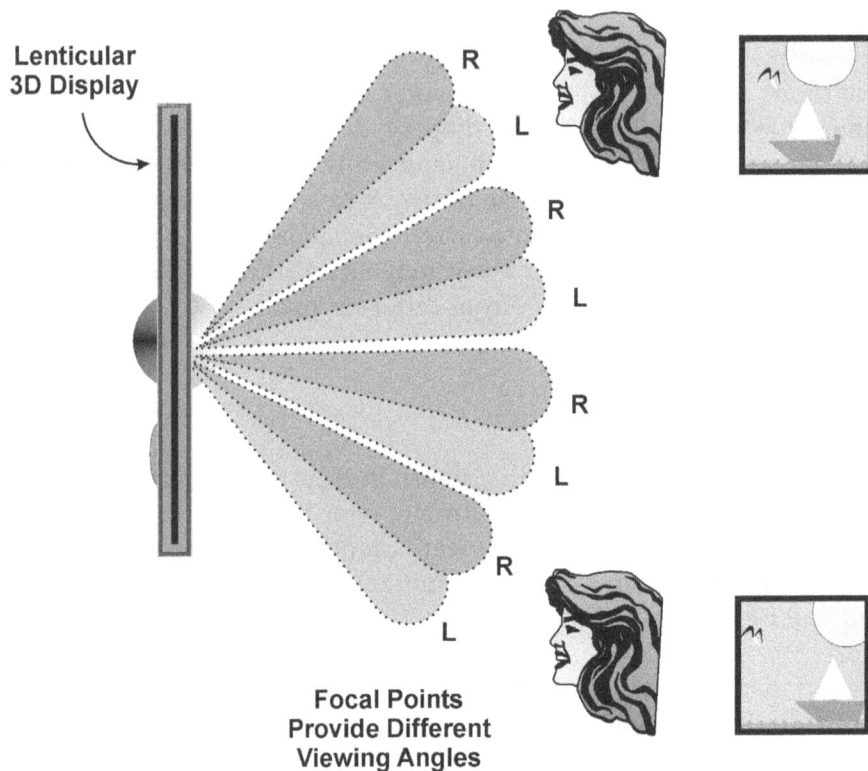

Lenticular 3D Display

R
L
R
L
R
L
R
L

Focal Points Provide Different Viewing Angles

Figure 1.17, Mutliview 3D Lenticular Display

Holographic

A hologram is a multi-dimensional images which allows a viewer to see the object at any angle. Holograms may be produced by lasers or through materials that bend, focus or redirect light. Using holographic transmission for videoconferencing is called telepresence.

Cable Telephony

Cable telephony is the providing of telephone services that use CATV systems to initiate, process, and receive voice communications. Cable telephony systems can either integrate telephony systems with cable modem networks (a teleservice) or the cable modem system can simply act as a transfer method for Internet telephony (bearer service).

Because of government regulations (restrictions or high operational level requirements) in many countries, some cable operators limit the integration of telephone services with their cable networks. In either case, cable telephony systems are data telephony systems that include a voice gateway, gatekeeper, and a media interface.

Voice over Internet Protocol (VoIP)

Voice Over Internet Protocol (VoIP) is a process of sending voice telephone signals over a data network that can use Internet protocol. If the telephone signal is in analog form (voice or fax) the signal is first converted to a digital form. Packet routing information is then added to the digital voice signal so it can be routed through the packet data network.

Voice Gateway

Voice gateway is a network device that converts communication signals between data networks and telephone networks. A gatekeeper is a server that translates dialed digits into routing points within the cable network or identifies a forwarding number for the public telephone network. A multi-media transfer adapter converts multiple types of input signals into a common communications format.

Multimedia Terminal Adapter (MTA)

A multimedia terminal adapter (MTA) is a device that is installed at the customer's location (their home) which can connect the subscriber's telephone line to the data network (such as the cable modem system). MTAs include the codecs and all signaling and encapsulation functions required for media transport (digital audio) and call signaling (e.g. dialing, call hold, and other features).

Figure 1.18 shows a CATV system that offers cable telephony services. This diagram shows that a two-way digital CATV system can be enhanced to offer cable telephony services by adding voice gateways to the cable network's head-end CMTS system and media terminal adapters (MTAs) at the residence or business. The voice gateway connects and converts signals from the public telephone network into data signals that can be transported on the cable modem system. The CMTS system uses a portion of the cable modem signal (data channel) to communicate with the MTA. The MTA converts the telephony data signal to its analog audio component for connection

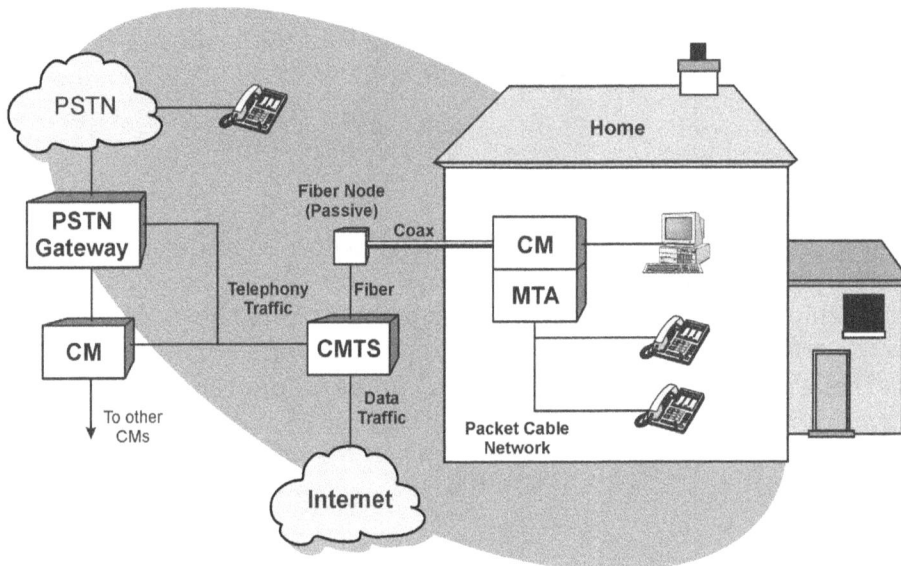

Figure 1.18, Cable Telephony

to standard telephones. MTAs are sometimes called integrated access devices (IADs).

Wireless Cable

Wireless Cable is a term given to land based (terrestrial) wireless distribution systems that utilize microwave frequencies to deliver video, data, and/or voice signals to end-users. There are two basic types of wireless cable systems; multichannel multipoint distribution service (MMDS) and local multichannel distribution service (LMDS).

The data-over-cable service interface specification (DOCSIS) with a few modifications can also be used in 2.6 GHz MMDS and 28 GHz LMDS systems [12]. This wireless standard is call DOCSIS+.

Wireless cable security can be provided using a wireless modem termination system (WMTS) which manages encryption keys and processes between the base station and end user devices.

Multichannel Multipoint Distribution Service (MMDS)

Multichannel multipoint distribution service is the providing of television services through the use of 2.5 GHz microwave frequencies. MMDS is commonly called "wireless cable" and is often used in rural areas to eliminate the cost of installing cable lines.

The relatively low MMDS microwave frequency permits its use from 10-20 miles. When using DOCSIS standards, MMDS frequencies can be shifted (down-converted) to work with standard TV set top boxes.

Local Multipoint Distribution Service (LMDS)

Local multipoint distribution service (LMDS) is a short range wireless communication service that operates between 28-31 GHz. Because LMDS high frequency is highly attenuated by water drops (rain fade), the maximum distance for LMDS connections is typically 1-2 miles. In 2015, the FCC issued a notice of proposed rulemaking (NPRM) to extend the frequency range into the 30 and 40 GHz bands [13].

Figure 1.19 shows an LMDS system. This diagram shows that the major component of a wireless cable system is the head-end equipment. The head-end building has a satellite connection for cable channels and video players for video on demand. The head-end is linked to base stations (BS) which transmits radio frequency signals for reception. An antenna and receiver in the home convert the microwave radio signals into the standard television channels for use in the home. As in traditional cable systems, a set-top box decodes the signal for input to the television. Low frequency wireless cable systems, such as MMDS wireless cable systems (approx 2.5 GHz), can reach up to approximately 70 miles. High frequency LMDS systems (approx 28 GHz) can only reach approximately 5 miles.

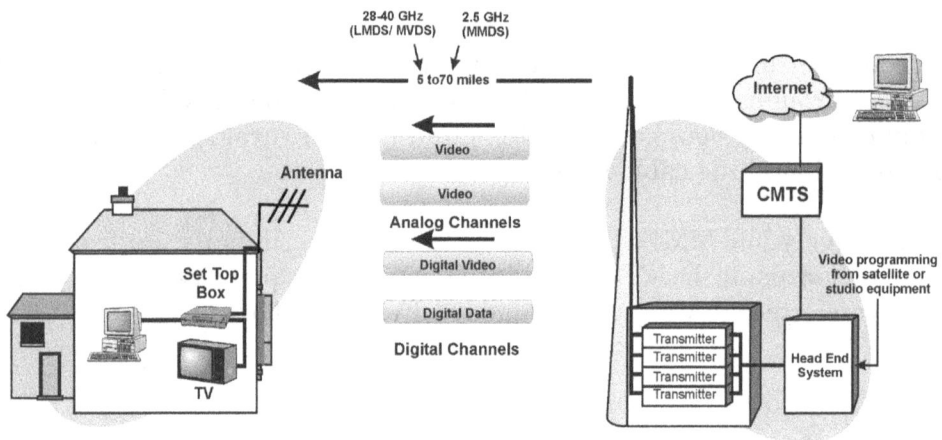

Figure 1.19, Local Multipoint Distribution System (LMDS)

Conditional Access Systems (CAS)

A conditional access system (CAS) is a security process that is used to limit the access of media (such as television channels or programs) to authorized users. Conditional access systems can use uniquely identifiable devices (sealed with serial numbers) and may use smart cards to store and access secret codes.

Content owners (such as movie studios and television networks) commonly require broadcasters to use CAS and guarantee that content distributed through their systems will only be delivered to authorized users and cannot be viewed or copied by unauthorized people.

To control access to content, the media that is broadcasted or streamed is modified (scrambled or encrypted). For recipients to be able to convert the media into its original form, the receiver needs to have keys and other information to decode the media. The encryption codes change over time (typically every few seconds). To receive the necessary decoding information, an additional stream (channel) of decoding information (entitlement messages) is transmitted along with the broadcasted media.

Content protection systems may also define the content access rules such as if the received media is authorized to be copied or what types of devices can view the media (such as standard or high definition televisions). Conditional access systems may be combined with additional content protection systems (such as home media distribution).

A downloadable conditional access system (DCAS) is a security process that is used in a communication system (such as a broadcast television system) to limit the access of media to authorized users that can be modified or updated.

Figure 1.20 shows that content protection in the home is an extension of content protection from other sources, including broadcast and stored media systems. The content from TV broadcasters is protected by conditional access (CA) systems through a set top box (STB). Content from stored media (DVDs, Blu-Ray) is protected by a content scrambling system. Content that is distributed through the home is protected by digital transmission content protection (DTCP) and high definition content protection (HDCP). Content that is stored by users is protected by content protection for recordable media (CPRM).

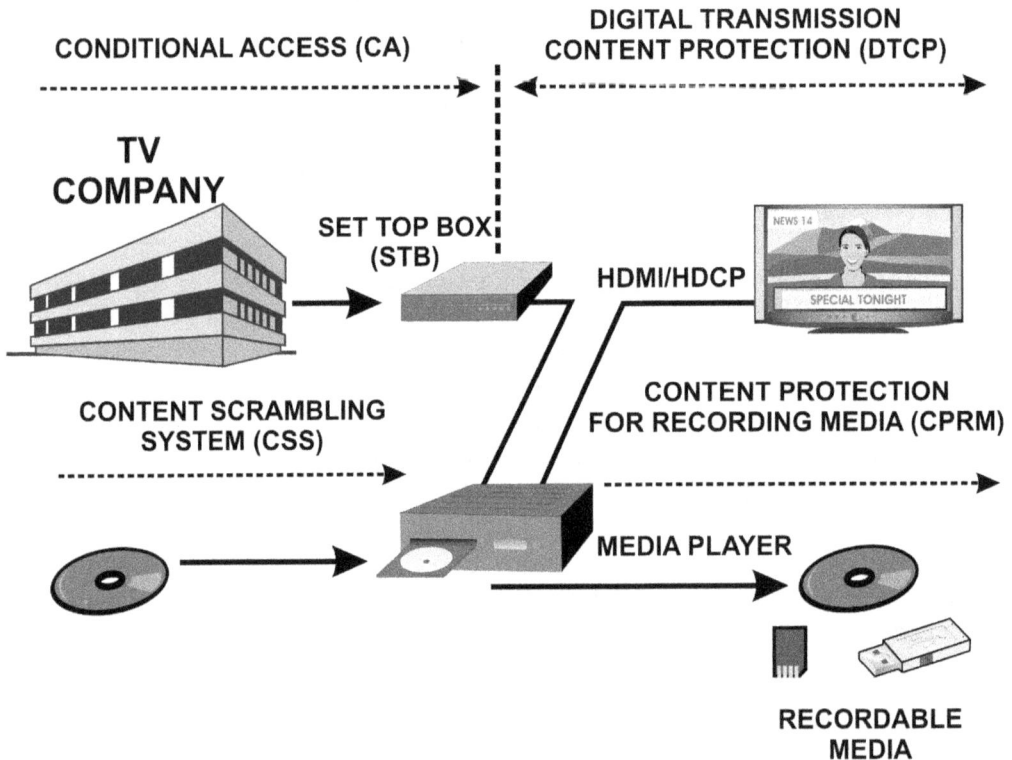

Figure 1.20, Conditional Access System (CAS)

Video on Demand (VoD)

Video on demand (VOD) is a service that allows customers to request and receive video services. The types of video on demand include near video on demand (NVOD), subscription video on demand (SVOD), advertising video on demand (AVOD), and transactional video on demand (TVOD.)

Near Video on Demand (NVOD)

Near video on demand is a video service that allows a customer to select from a limited number of broadcast video channels. These video channels are typically movie channels that have pre-designated schedule times. Unlike full VOD service, the customer is not able to alter the start or play time of these broadcast videos.

Subscription Video on Demand (SVOD)

Subscription video on demand (SVOD) enables pre-registered audiences to select and watch videos from a predetermined list of video programs. Registered subscribers typically pay a recurring fee for access to any of the programming. Content providers may receive a fixed revenue for each show provided for a time period (such as monthly) and/or may receive a percentage of subscription revenue based on the amount of viewing time.

Advertising Video on Demand (AVOD)

Advertising video on demand service allows audiences to have free access to content that includes advertising messages. Content providers typically receive a percentage of advertising revenue generated by audience viewing. AVOD may highly target ads by viewer profiles and behaviors earning much higher revenues than traditional broadcast advertising. AVOD service may require the viewer to watch ads without the ability to skip or fast forward through the TV commercials.

Transactional Video on Demand (TVOD)

Transactional video on demand allows viewers to request and pay for access to programs for a fee. Content providers typically receive a percentage of revenue generated by audience pay per view (PPV) access purchases.

Figure 1.21 shows key types of video on demand services. Near video on demand (NVOD) service allows viewers to access specific channels or programs during prescheduled times. Subscription video on demand (SVOD) service allows pre-registered audiences access to all programs in on demand library. Advertising video on demand (AVOD) provides viewers with free access to content that includes advertising messages. Transactional video on demand (TVOD) allows viewers to purchase access or time periods to view programs.

Service	Description	Content Revenue (typical)
Near Video on Demand (NVOD)	Prescheduled Times, Access Provided during Time Periods	Transaction Revenue Share
Subscription Video on Demand (SVOD)	Pre-Registered Audiences Access to all Programs in Library	Fixed Revenue for each Show Licensed, Subscription Revenue Share by Viewing Time
Advertising Video on Demand (AVOD)	Free Access to Content which Includes Advertising Messages	Advertising Revenue Share
Transactional Video on Demand (TVOD)	Pay per View or Access Time Period	Transaction Revenue Share

Figure 1.21, Video on Demand (VOD) Types

Interactive Television (iTV)

Interactive television is a combination of cable, television, multimedia, PCs, and network programming that allows dynamic control of media display using inputs from the end-user. Interactive TV uses real time connections to provide enhanced content when certain conditions (triggers) occur.

Real Time Connections

Real time connections for Internet TV can be provided by the cable system as a DOCSIS channel or by an Internet connection (which is transferred by a DOCSIS connection). Most CATV systems use Internet connections to transfer media and data such as program guides or set top box software updates.

Enhanced Content

Enhanced content is the sending of additional data or signals along with media that can enhance the viewing or usage experience. An example is the sending of video clips that will be displayed in certain areas of the screen based on options the viewer chooses. Enhanced content may not require a return channel to confirm the reception or interaction with the enhanced television (ETV) programs.

Examples of interactive TV content that has been used include comments, polls, questions, and other types of audience responses to program content.

Application Programs

Application programs (Apps) are software files that contains commands that can process media and data. Application programs may be independent of the program being viewed (unbound) or may be bound (linked) to a program file. An unbound application could be a TV navigation guide that can be activated at any time. A bound application could be a voting option for a segment within a show or movie.

Television Applications (TV Apps)

Television apps are independent software applications that can be added to TV systems to provide new features and services. Some types of TV apps include news widgets, weather apps, and product apps. These apps may process information that can be display on or within the video display.

Some connected TV devices such as Blu-Ray players, Smart TVs, and gaming consoles are able to use and process TV applications such as video apps such as NetFlix, Amazon Prime, Hulu, and other services.

App Software Language

The software languages used for TV apps range from HTML5, Java (Android), variations of XML (Roku), custom languages such as Swift from Apple.

Installation and Downloading

TV app programs may be preloaded (installed) at the manufacturing facility or may be downloaded after the user has setup the device. While some TV App may be sold, a majority of apps are provided at no cost to enable users to have access to subscription services or in-App purchases.

Figure 1.22 shows how advertising TV apps can be downloaded and activated in a viewer's set top box when certain conditions occur. This diagram shows that a TV app program is loaded which displays a real estate agents offer to provide a buyer's tip sheet is activated when a viewer selects a real estate TV program. When the viewer presses the "Select" button on their remote control, they will be given the option to receive the tips by email or by mail.

1. **Download TV Widget Program**

2. **Run TV Widget**

STB Memory layers:

Layer	Function
TV Widget Program	Graphics and Interaction
Application Interface	Interpretation
Operating System (OS)	Operation Processing
Driver	Adapt/Interface

STB Memory

Real Estate

Free Home Buyer TIPS!
PRESS "SELECT"

4. **Widget Program Displays Ad**

3. **Viewer Changes to Real Estate Channel (triggers TV widget)**

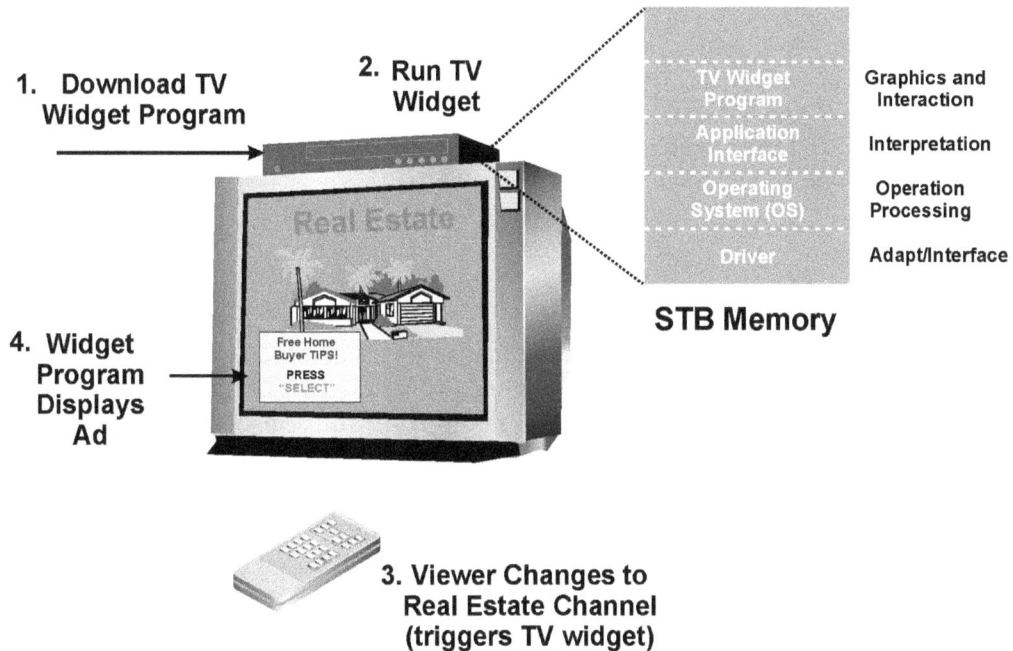

Figure 1.22, Television Apps

Internet Protocol Television (IPTV)

Internet protocol television (IPTV) is the process of providing television (video and/or audio) services through the use Internet protocol (IP) networks. IPTV networks initiate, process, and receive voice or multimedia communications using IP protocol. These IP systems may be public IP systems (e.g. the Internet), private data systems (e.g. telephone system DSL network), or a hybrid of public and private systems.

Switched Video

Switched video service (SVS) is the process that can dynamically setup (on demand) video signal connections between two or more points. SVS services can range from the setup of data connections that allow video transfer to the organization and management of video content and the delivery of video programs.

IP Data Networks

Internet protocol data networks use address and control information in each packet to direct (forward) packets towards their destination in the network. Each IP packet header contains addressing information (source and destination address) and basic control information (such as time to live). Additional headers (such as a TCP header) contain control or additional routing information (such as a port number) related to a specific application for which the packet is related to. The data portion of the datagram has a variable length.

Data Multicasting

Data multicasting is the process of transmitting a single stream of packets (a media channel) to multiple destinations by using packet switches (multicast routers) that can copy and redistribute packets to multiple ports. Data multicasting makes broadcasting through packet data networks more efficient by setting up distribution trees (copy and redistribute branches) using routers.

Internet TV (OTT)

An Internet TV system provides video and audio (television) media on a communication channel that is delivered through the public Internet. These television signals can be viewed in computers, standard televisions (using an adapter), connected TVs (smart televisions), or other types of multimedia devices that can receive streaming video signals (such as game consoles). Internet TV is sometimes referred to as over the top television (OTT) because the TV signals travel over the top of the Internet rather than through a broadcast television system.

Because Internet TV signals can reach many types of connected devices located almost anywhere, virtually any company or person can become a global television provider. Internet TV systems are similar to regular broadcast television stations, except they send TV signals through the Internet and can be combined with additional media processing and interactive features (Internet TV+).

Internet TV Content Sources

Internet TV content sources can range from live TV networks (such as Fox or CNN) to niche, on-demand content from micro-producers. Internet TV systems can deliver an unlimited number of channels as each television set only requires one TV channel connection. Each connection can be linked to any other TV source the Internet TV service operator (broadcaster) can and is willing to provide.

Internet TV Service Providers

Internet TV service providers, also called online video providers (OVP), obtain the rights to transmit media programming to people that they allow to view their signals (free and/or paying subscribers). While Internet TV service providers may focus on providing TV services in geographic areas (such as where they own or control TV distribution rights), they can technically provide and restrict programming anywhere they can reach customers through a broadband data connection.

Internet TV Distribution Systems

Internet TV distribution systems transfer media programs from content sources to viewing devices. There are many types of systems that can distribute IP data packets, including telecom, wireless, cable TV systems, power companies (data over power line), and competitive access providers (such as new optical networks).

Internet TV provides may own or use content distribution networks (CDN) for Internet TV distribution. Connections in CDNs may be able to be controlled to ensure accurate distribution timing. This is important for the providing of live content (such as sports) so viewed broadcast programs (such as the superbowl) can be presented at the same time as streaming TV viewers.

Internet TV Viewing Devices

Internet TV viewing devices can receive media in Internet Protocol (IP) packet format and convert it into media that can be viewed by users. IP viewing devices range from standard televisions that use digital media adapter boxes to convert IP video signals, to smart mobile telephones with digital video viewing capabilities.

Figure 1.23 shows that Internet TV systems are composed of content providers, broadband Internet connections, video viewing devices and Internet TV service providers. The content providers include existing television networks, on demand content providers (content aggregators), and independent content provider companies. This example shows a distribution networks that uses many types of systems to transfer IP video packets from the content source to the viewing devices. IPTV viewing devices include standard televisions (with adapters), multimedia computers and multimedia mobile devices. The Internet TV system operator manages how customers can connect to the system and which services they can receive.

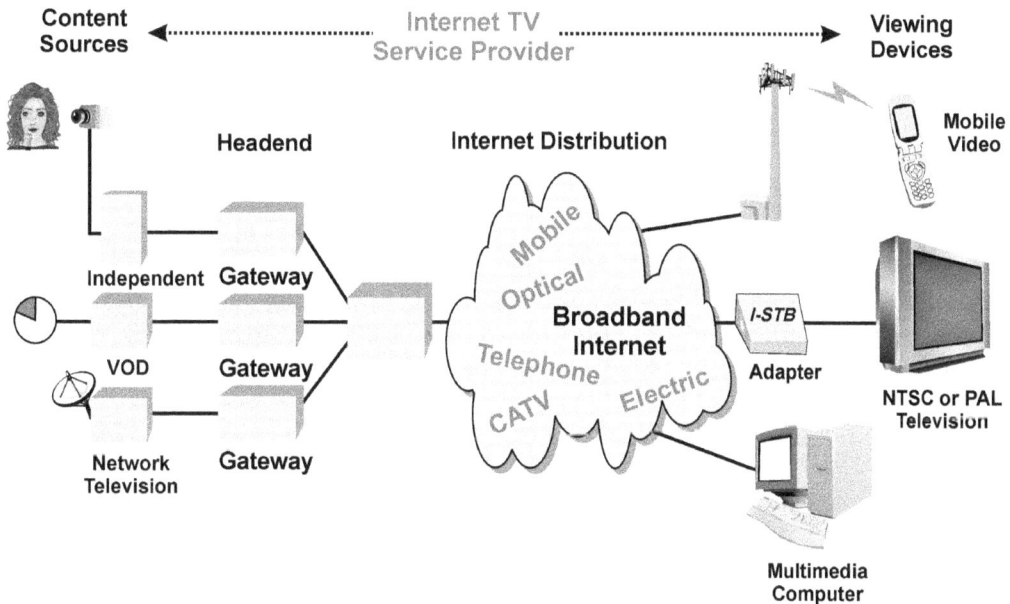

Figure 1.23, Basic Internet TV System

Hybrid TV

Hybrid TV systems provide multiple types of content sources such as broadcast TV (wireless), cable TV, satellite, and Internet TV to reach a single user and interact with each other. The media programs are combined in a single electronic program guide (EPG). Media programs from one or more of the media sources may include enhanced content that allows viewers to interact with the movies and shows.

Multiple Media Sources

Hybrid TV systems allows viewers to receive signals from multiple broadcast and media sources. This can include broadcast TV, satellite TV, Cable TV, and IPTV, and Internet TV (OTT).

Integrated Program Guide

Hybrid TV systems use one program guide that displays information from two or more media sources. The information in the program guide may be reorganized by categories or other viewer preferences.

Interactive Services

Hybrid TV may provide programs that contain enhanced content (links and media) that can customize the content (e.g. replacing sport team logos with preferred viewer logos) and provide interaction capabilities (media and feature selection, polls, and applications.)

Figure 1.24 shows a hybrid TV system that can receive programs from satellite, broadcast TV, cable TV, and Internet TV. The program information from each of these sources is combined into an integrated electronic program guide (EPG). Programs that received from the media sources also contain enhanced content (links and media) that can personalize viewer content and allow for viewers to Interact through an Internet return connection.

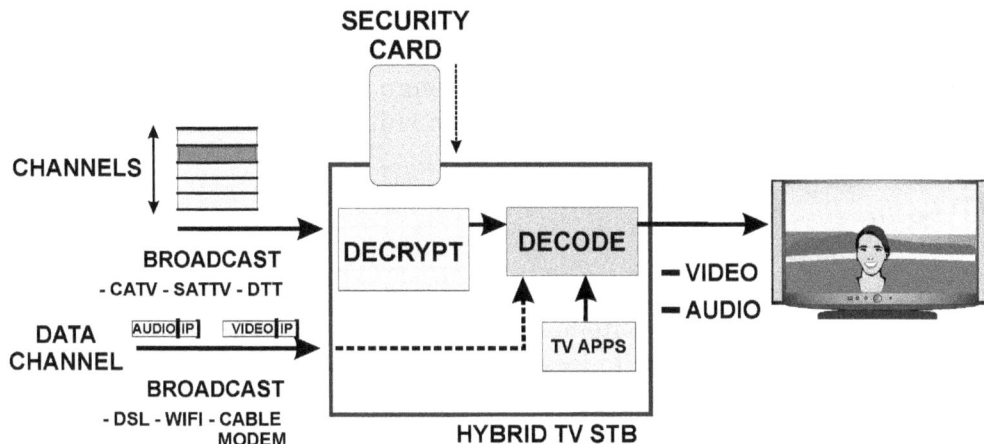

Figure 1.24, Hybrid TV System

Social TV

Social TV is the combination of TV systems with social networks. Social TV systems can add Internet content references to programs, set up and monitor viewer communication (backchannels), and produces new media which can be sent with the TV programs or shared with other media channels. Social networks add new content tagging types, hosts new groups, and coordinates media sharing between members. The combined system increases TV reach (via shares and recommendations), improves the viewing experience (additional content), and provides immediate response channels for advertising (amazing revenue multiplier).

Broadcast systems transmit media that have high production value - it looks like TV or movie content. Broadcasters add social TV to their systems by updating program content (inserting social tags and references), creates new content (for second screen and media channels), and by providing new direct communication services (recommending and sharing TV programs).

Social networks provide services that allow people and groups to publish and share content. Social networks add social TV to their systems by adding new types of tags, directly tying into TV systems (with direct API and indirect soft connections), and by creating and managing groups (fan clubs) that can share and process rich media (program snippets and commentary).

TV Social References

TV social references are the direct or indirect inclusion of web addresses, media tags, or other media items into movies or shows that provides and encourages the viewer to go to locations on the Internet.

Direct references may be a text URL, hashtag, or other identifier that is displayed in the video which a viewer can use to find additional information on the web. Indirect references can be the inclusion of identifiers and calls to action in scripts such. For example, the reference to get more information about "ProfessorBedlam.com" in Super Ex Girlfriend produced by Regency films distributed by 20th Century Fox (which is registered to Fox Film but not in use at the time this book was produced.)

The addition of TV social references can result in production and creative director conflicts. This is leading to Social TV producers and directors who balance between creative content with social media needs.

New Social TV Content

Social TV content includes inserting social media items into TV programs, creating second screen content, and producing collateral content for social media channels.

Gathering content from social networks involves content mediation. This includes requesting, organizing, rating, getting permission, and formatting media so it can be inserted into TV program. Insertion may be at pre-designated insertion points in the TV content or determined by a live social TV director. This can include responses to live social media polls (voting using Twitter), showing submitted posts, photos, and videos.

Second screen content can be a mix of simulcast transmission (program simultaneously displayed on second screen) and collateral content. Ads on second screen may be enhanced or replaced with other commercials. The value of commercials that simultaneously appear on the second screen at the same time (synchronized ads) can be much higher as they can enable real time response from the viewers.

Collateral content can be published on media channels such as online fan clubs. This includes clips from the TV program, out takes, and related programming.

Media Channels (Backchannels)

TV backchannels are communication channels that can be used by viewers to directly communicate with the TV system or share information about the TV program. Managing backchannels includes monitoring, publishing, and engaging with viewers.

Backchannels have been available since the beginning of television. Fan mail and fan clubs have and continue to provide feedback to the producers and networks. Social TV provides a more effective and engaging backchannel platform.

Monitoring involves continually reviewing key media channels for mentions and content that is related to TV programs. Monitoring can range from setting up simple Google alerts to track program and actor names to using advanced sentiment analysis tools to track key trends.

Backchannel publishing involves releasing program or related media to backchannels. This includes selecting program segments which the content owner is willing to allow social distribution (traditionally movie trailers). Additional content can be released including out takes, event schedules, and content provided by the actors.

The management of backchannel engagement involves using hosts and agents who can engage with the audience. TV show or network channels owners may manage these channels and provide a host or moderator that coordinates the media and engages with the audience.

A key benefit (and growing concern) is measurement of viewer engagement. While Nielsen ratings measurements provides the number of viewers, social TV ratings measure the actual audience interests and engagement levels. This can dramatically influence what advertisers are willing to pay for TV spots. Some of the social TV ratings services include Nielsen Social, Rentrak, and Kantar Media. To get an updated list of social TV ratings services, go to:

Nielsen Social - http://www.nielsensocial.com/
Rentrak - http://www.rentrak.com/
Kantar Media - http://www.kantarmedia.com

Social Network Connections

Setting up social network connections can involve setting up direct application program interface (API) connections between TV systems or creating soft relationships between social network members and groups.

Direct API connections between TV systems and social networks allow for real time interaction. API connection can enable live polling responses to contests through TV devices (such as the TV remote control) or connected devices (smartphone or tablet).

TV systems may setup indirect connections through monitoring and engagement channels. To create indirect soft connections, social groups can be monitored for reference word and phrases and members can be engaged using an agent of the show.

Figure 1.25 shows a social TV platform that ties a TV broadcasting system to a social network system. The TV broadcast content is enhanced by adding references to Internet content such as web addresses or indirect displays or mentions of Internet content. The TV broadcaster has also created new collateral content that is sent to a second screen viewing device (tablet) which is connected to the Internet. The tablet can receive the synchronized content while and also access social network groups and Internet content. This TV system has additional two-way communication capabilities that allows the viewer to directly interact with content using their TV remote control (rate, bookmark, share, and comment). Viewers and other people can send messages and content to the TV system via the social network which can be used to enhance or produce new TV content (including photos and videos in TV content). Viewers can also communicate with the TV media channels (fan clubs) and other groups through their social network accounts.

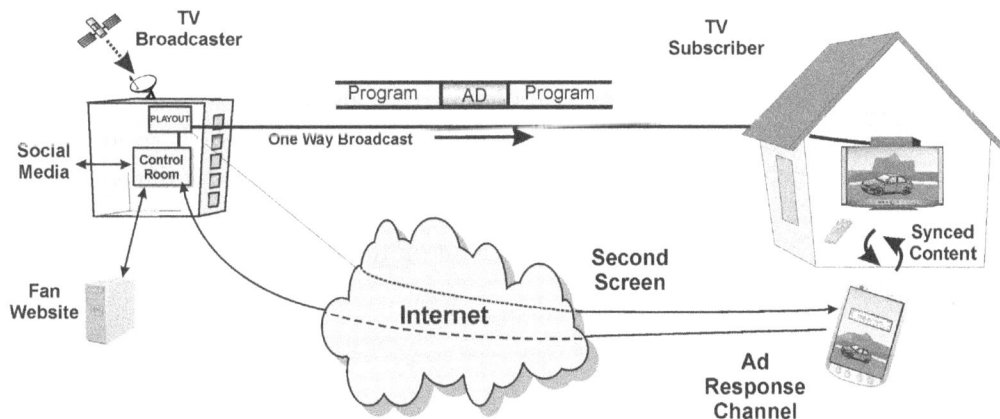

Figure 1.25, Social TV System

Contribution Network

A contribution network is a system that interconnects content sources (media programs) to a content user (e.g. a television system). CATV systems receive content from multiple sources through connections that range from dedicated high-speed fiber optic connections to the delivery of stored media. Content sources include program networks, content aggregators and a variety of other government, educational and public sources.

Content Feeds

A content feed is a media source that comes from a content provider or stored media system. The types of content feeds that may be used in CATV systems range from network feeds (popular programming) to video feeds from public events (government programming).

Off Air Feed

An off air feed is a content source that comes from an antenna system that captures programming from broadcasted radio signals (off air radio transmission). The off air feed converts broadcasted radio channels into a format that can be retransmitted on another system (such as a CATV system). Off-air feeds are used to retransmit locally broadcasted content on the CATV system.

Network Feed

A network feed is a media connection that is used to transfer media or programs from a network to a distributor of the media or programs.

Local Feed

A local feed is a media connection that is used to transfer content from local sources. Examples of local feeds include connection from sportscasts, news crews and live studio cameras.

Truck Feed

A truck feed is a media connection that is used to transfer content from mobile news vehicle source. Examples of truck feeds include cellular and microwave connections.

Helicopter Feed

A helicopter feed is a media connection that is used to transfer content from airborne sources. Examples of helicopter feeds include microwave and private radio connections.

Live Feed

A live feed is a media connection that is used to transfer media or programs from a device that is capturing in real time (such as a mobile camera) to a distributor of the media or programs.

Government Access Channel

A government access channel is a media source that is dedicated to informing citizens of public related information. Examples of government programming include legal announcements, property zoning, public worker training programs, election coverage, health related disease controls and other public information that is related to citizens.

Educational Access Channel

An educational access channel is a media source that is dedicated to education. Educational programming may come from public or private schools. Examples of educational programming include student programming, school sporting events, distance learning classes, student artistic performances and the viewpoints and teachings of instructors.

Public Access Channel

A public access channel is a media source that is dedicated to allowing the public to create and provide programming to a broadcast system. Examples of public programming include local events and subjects that members of a community have an interest in.

Syndication Feeds

Syndication feeds are media connections or sources that are used to transfer media or programs from a syndicated network to a distributor of the media or programs. An example of a syndicated feed is really simple syndication (RSS) feed. An RSS feed provides content via the Internet such as news stories. RSS allows content from multiple sources to be more easily distributed. RSS content feeds are often commonly identified on web sites by an orange rectangular icon.

Emergency Alert System (EAS)

An emergency alert system is a system that coordinates the sending of messages to broadcast networks of cable networks, AM, FM, and TV broadcast stations; Low Power TV (LPTV) stations and other communications providers during public emergencies. When emergency alert signals are received, the transmission of broadcasting equipment is temporarily shifted to emergency alert messages.

Figure 1.26 shows some of the different types of content sources that may be gathered through a contribution network. This table shows that content sources include off-air local programs, entertainment from national networks, local programs, government access (public information), education access, public access (residents), syndication (shared sources), and the emergency alert systems.

Content Sources	Notes
Off-air feed	Local programs
Network feed	Entertainment and nationwide programs
Local feed	Local information
Truck feed	Event and news information
Helicopter feed	Traffic and news
Live feed	Local news
Government access channel	Public information
Education access channel	Schools and learning sources
Public access channel	Community residents
Syndication feeds	News and shared resources
Emergency alert system	Public safety

Figure 1.26, Contribution Network Programming Sources

Contribution Connection Types

CATV contribution network connection types include satellite connections, leased lines, virtual networks, microwave links, mobile data systems, and public data networks (e.g. Internet).

Satellite Distribution

Content distributors that provide television programming to CATV networks via satellite lease some or all of the transponder capacity of the satellite. Satellite content providers combine multiple programs (channels) for distribution to broadcasters.

Satellite communication is the use of orbiting satellites to relay communications signals from one station to many others. A satellite communication link includes a communication link that passes through several types of systems. These connections include the transmission electronics and antenna, uplink path, satellite reception and transmission equipment (transponder), downlink path, and reception electronics and antenna. Because satellite systems provide signal coverage to a wide geographic area, the high cost of satellites can be shared by many broadcasting companies.

Leased Line

Leased lines are telecommunication lines or links that have part or all of their transmission capacity dedicated (reserved) to the exclusive use of a single customer or company. Leased lines often come with a guaranteed level of performance for connections between two points. Leased lines may be used to guarantee the transfer of media at specific times.

Virtual Private Network (VPN)

Virtual private networks are assigned communication path(s) within a system that transfer data or information through one or more data networks that are dedicated between two or more points. VPN connections allow data to safely and privately pass over public networks (such as the Internet). The data traveling between two points is usually encrypted for privacy. Virtual private networks allow the cost of a public communication system to be shared by multiple companies.

Mobile Data

Mobile data is the transmission of digital information through a wireless network (such as a 3G or 4G mobile telephone system) in which the communication equipment can move or be located over a relatively wide geographic area. In general, the use of mobility in data communication results in an increased cost for data transmission.

Because mobile data transmission data speeds can be low, transmitters that send television signals over multiple networks may use and combine multiple phones (inverse multiplexing.)

Internet

is a public data network that interconnects private and government computers together. The Internet transfers data from point to point by packets that use Internet protocol (IP). Each transmitted packet in the Internet finds its way through the network switching through nodes (computers). Each node in the Internet forwards received packets to another location (another node) that is closer to its destination. Each node contains routing tables that provide packet forwarding information. The Internet can be effectively used to privately transfer programs through the use of encryption.

Microwave Link

Microwave links use frequencies above 1 GHz for line of sight radio communications (20 to 30 miles) between two directional antennas. Each microwave link transceiver usually offers a standard connection to communication networks such as a T1/E1 or DS3 connection line. This use of microwave links eliminates the need to install cables between communication equipment. Microwave links may be licensed (filed and protected by government agencies) or may be unlicensed (through the use of low power within unlicensed regulatory limits). Microwave links are commonly used by CATV systems to connect remote devices or locations, such as a mobile news truck or a helicopter feed.

Stored Media

In additional to gathering content through communication links, content may be gathered through the use of stored media. Examples of stored media include portable hard disks, magnetic tapes (VHS or Beta) and optical disks (CD or DVDs).

Figure 1.27 shows a contribution network that is used with a CATV system. This example shows that programming that is gathered through a contribution network can come from a variety of sources that include satellite connections, leased lines, virtual networks, microwave links, mobile data, public data networks (e.g. Internet) and the use of stored media (tapes and DVDs).

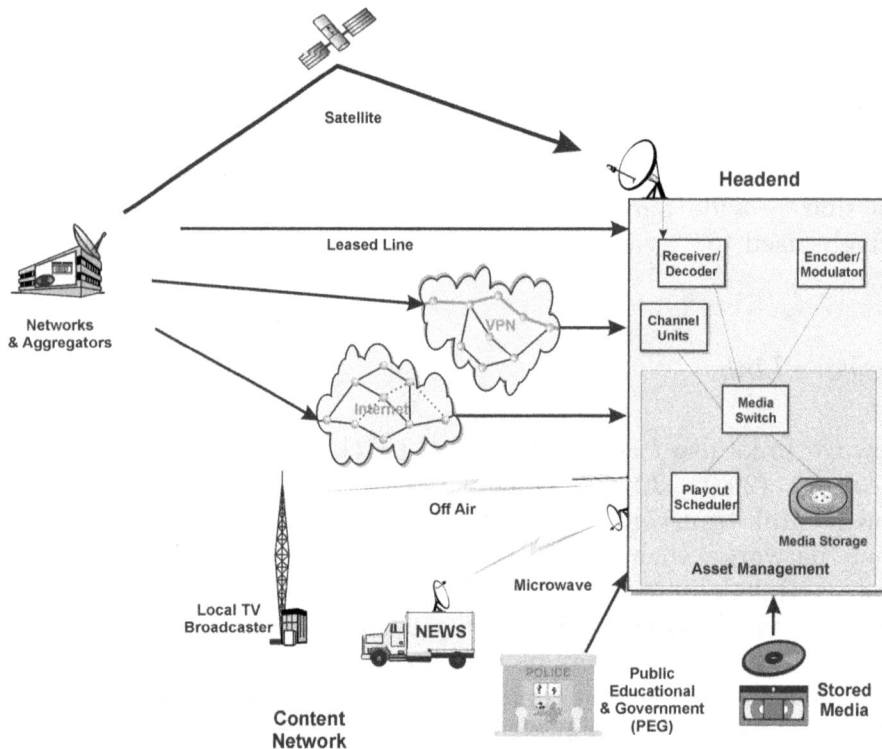

Figure 1.27, Contribution Network

Program Transfer Scheduling

Program transfer scheduling is the setup and management of the times and connection types by which media will be transported to the CATV system. CATV systems have a limited amount of media storage for television programs, so they typically schedule the transfer programming a short time (possibly several days) before it will be broadcasted by their systems.

Program Transfer Cost

The cost of transferring content can vary based on the connection type (e.g. satellite versus Internet) and the data transfer speed. In general, the faster the data transfer speed, the higher the transfer cost. The scheduling of program transfer during low network capacity usage periods and at lower speeds can result in significant reductions in transfer cost.

Figure 1.28 shows how a CATV system may use transfer scheduling to obtain programs reliably and cost effectively. This example shows that the CATV system may select multiple connection types and transfer speeds. This diagram shows that the selection can depend on the program type (live versus scheduled) and transfer cost.

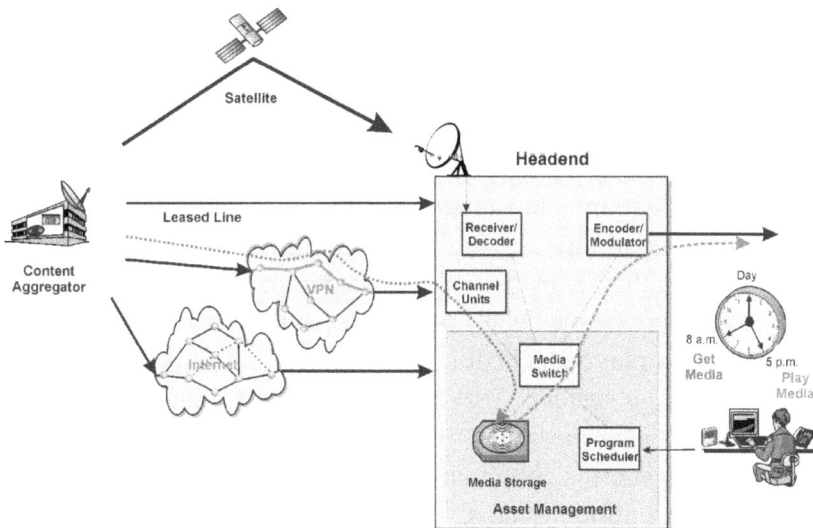

Figure 1.28, CATV Program Transfer Scheduling

Media Asset Management (MAM)

Media asset management (also called content asset management - CAM) is the process of acquiring, maintaining, distributing and eliminating movies, shows, graphics, and other media items. Assets are managed by workflow systems. Workflow management for television systems involves content acquisition, metadata management, asset storage, playout scheduling, content processing, ad insertion and distribution control.

Content Assets

Content assets are acquired or created. Each asset is given an identification code and descriptive data (metadata) and the licensing usage terms and costs are associated with the asset.

Assets are transferred into short term or long term storage systems that allow the programs to be retrieved when needed. Schedules (program bookings) are setup to retrieve the assets from storage shortly before they are to be broadcasted to viewers. When programs are broadcasted, they are converted (encoded) into forms that are suitable for transmission (such as on radio broadcast channels or to mobile telephones).

Figure 1.29 shows some of the common steps that occur in workflow management systems. This diagram shows that a workflow management system starts with gathering content and identifying its usage rights. The descriptive metadata for the programs is then managed and the programs are stored in either online (direct), nearline (short delay) or offline (long term) storage systems. Channel and program playout schedules are created and setup. As programs are transferred from storage systems, they may be processed and converted into other formats. Advertising messages may be inserted into the programs. The performance of the system is continually monitored as programs are transmitted `through the distribution systems.

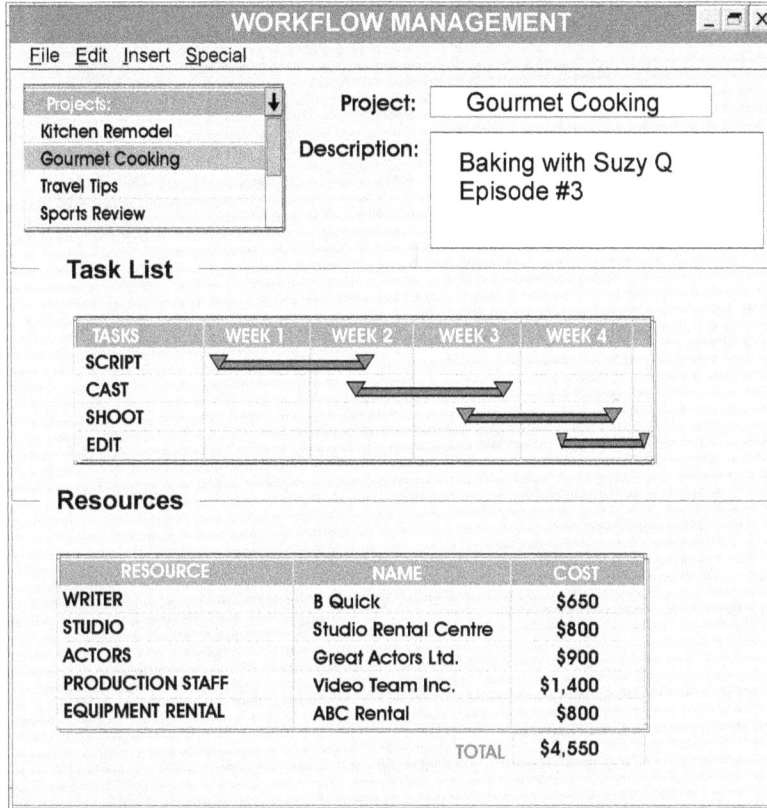

Figure 1.29, Television Workflow Management Systems

Content Production

Cable TV systems content production options typically include public access content, TV commercials, and local content.

Public, Education, and Government (PEG)

Public, Education, and Government (PEG) is public access programming. Cable TV operators may be required to allow residents access to create and broadcast public content on the cable TV system as part of cable TV system franchise distribution agreement. The franchise agreement provides the cable TV provider with the right to install cables to homes in the area.

In addition to providing access to broadcast channels, cable TV operators may be required to provide training and access to production equipment (cameras, video editors, studios.) There are restrictions on the types of content and business promotion activities for public TV producers. The training educates residents in what they are allowed to produce and how they are allowed to use the content they create.

Local Content

Cable TV operators may original content local news, cover local events, or sponsored activities. Cable TV systems typically have a production studio and news truck(s) for local event coverage and electronic news gathering (ENG.)

TV Commercial Production

Cable TV companies may produce or use media agencies to produce TV commercials for local advertisers. Their TV production services may be created at low or no cost to entice advertisers to purchase advertising campaigns. Cable TV companies may use templates or stock media to help reduce the cost of TV commercial production.

When cable TV companies use media agencies for TV commercial production, a percentage of the advertising fees (agency discount) may be provided back to the agency (typically 15% to 20%). The advertiser is invoiced for media time (ad insertions) and the media agency receives the commission separately so the advertiser may think that they do not pay an agency commission.

Content Acquisition

Content acquisition is the gathering of content from networks, aggregators and other sources. After content is acquired (or during the content transfer), content is ingested (adapted and stored) into the asset management system.

Ingestion

Ingesting content is a process by which content is acquired (e.g. from a satellite downlink or a data connection) and loaded onto initial video servers (ingest servers). Once content is ingested it can be edited to add commercials, migrated to a playout server or played directly into the transmission chain.

Licensing Terms

Content acquisition commonly involves applying a complex set of content licensing requirements, restrictions and associated costs to the content. These licensing terms are included in content distribution agreements.

Usage Limitations

Content licensing terms may define the specific types of systems (e.g. cable, Internet or mobile video), the geographic areas in which the content may be broadcasted (territories), the types of viewers (residential or commercial), and specific usage limitations (such as number of times a program can be broadcasted in a month). The content acquisition system is linked to a billing system to calculate the royalties and other costs for the media.

Metadata Management

Metadata management is the process of identifying, describing and applying rules to the descriptive portions (metadata) of content assets. Cable TV system metadata may be asset IDs, titles, categories, descriptions, or other information about channels, programs, or media items (logos, video clips, etc).

Metadata Uses

Metadata may be used to create and supplement the electronic programming guide (EPG). An EPG is an interface (portal) that allows a customer to preview and select from a possible list of available content media. EPGs can vary from simple program selection to interactive filters that dynamically allow the user to filter through program guides by theme, time period, or other criteria.

Metadata Sources

Metadata may come from content owners, movie and show distributors, or 3rd party information providers. Key TV metadata providers include Tribune Media, Gemstar-TV (Rovi), and FYI Television.

Metadata Normalization

Metadata descriptions and formats can vary so metadata may be normalized. Metadata normalization is the adjustment of metadata elements into standard terms and formats to allow for more reliable organization, selection and presentation of program descriptive elements.

Playout Scheduling

Playout scheduling is the process of setting up the event times to transfer media or programs to viewers or distributors of the media. A playout system is an equipment or application that can initiate, manage and terminate the gathering, transferring or streaming of media to users or distributors of the media at a predetermined time schedule or when specific criteria have been met.

Time Slot Assignment

Playout systems are used to select and assign programs (digital assets) to time slots on linear television channels. Playout systems are used to setup playlists that can initiate automatic playout of media during scheduled interviews or alert operators to manually setup and start the playout of media programs (e.g. taps or DVDs).

Playout Event Selection

Playout systems may be capable of selecting primary and secondary events. Primary events are the programs that will be broadcasted and secondary events are media items that will be combined or used with the primary event. Examples of secondary events include logo insertion, text crawls (scrolling text), voice over (e.g. narrative audio clips) and special effects (such as a squeeze back).

Playout Automation

Because the number of channels and programs is increasing, broadcasters may use playout automation to reduce the effort required (workload) to setup play-out schedules. Playout automation is the process of using a system that has established rules or procedures that allows for the streaming or transferring of media to a user or distributor of the media at a predetermined time, schedule or when specific criteria have been met (such as user registration and payment).

Figure 1.30 shows that playout scheduling involves selecting programs and assigning playout times. This diagram shows a playout system that has multiple linear television channels and that events are setup to gather and playout media programs.

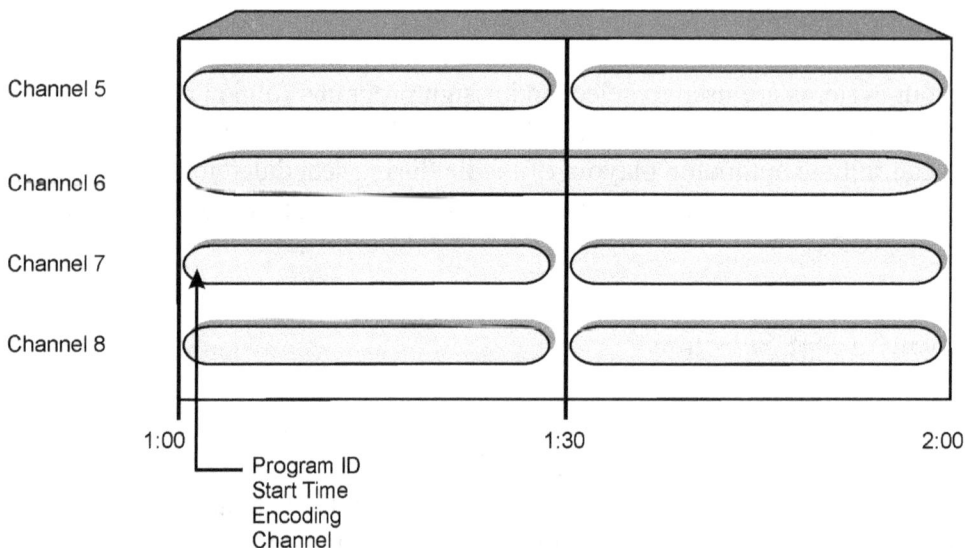

Figure 1.30, Television Playout Scheduling

Asset Storage

Asset storage is the maintenance of valuable and identifiable data or media (e.g. television program assets) in media storage devices and systems. Asset storage systems may use a combination of analog and digital storage media and these may be directly or indirectly accessible to the asset management system.

Asset management systems commonly use several types of storage devices that have varying access types, storage and transfer capabilities. Analog television storage systems may include tape cartridge (magnetic tape) storage. Digital storage systems include magnetic tape, removable and fixed disks and electronic memory.

Asset storage devices are commonly setup in a hierarchical structure to enable the coordination of media storage. Some of the different types of storage systems include cache storage (high speed immediate access), online storage, nearline storage, and offline storage.

Online Storage

Online storage is a device or system that stores data that is directly and immediately accessible by other devices or systems. Online storage types can vary from disk drives to electronic memory modules. Media may be moved from one type of online storage system to another type of online storage system (such as a disk drive) to another type of online storage system (such as electronic memory), which would allow for rapid access and caching. Caching is a process by which information is moved to a temporary storage area to assist in the processing or future transfer of information to other parts of a processor or system.

Nearline Storage

Nearline storage is a device or system that stores data or information that is accessible with some connection setup processes and/or delays. The requirement to find and/or setup a connection to media or information on a nearline storage system is relatively small. Data or media that is scheduled to be transmitted (e.g. broadcasted) may be moved to nearline storage before it is moved to an online storage system.

Offline Storage

Offline storage is a device or system that stores data or information that is not immediately accessible. Media in offline storage systems must be located and setup in order for connection or transfer to be obtained. Examples of offline storage systems include storage tapes and removable disks.

Figure 1.31 shows a TV system that contains multiple types of media storage systems. Online media storage (high-speed disk drives) store programs that can be immediately access for playing. Nearline media storage (network connected storage) can transfer media programs after they have been identified and to. Offline storage systems contain media (such as DVDs) that must be physically accessed so it can be used.

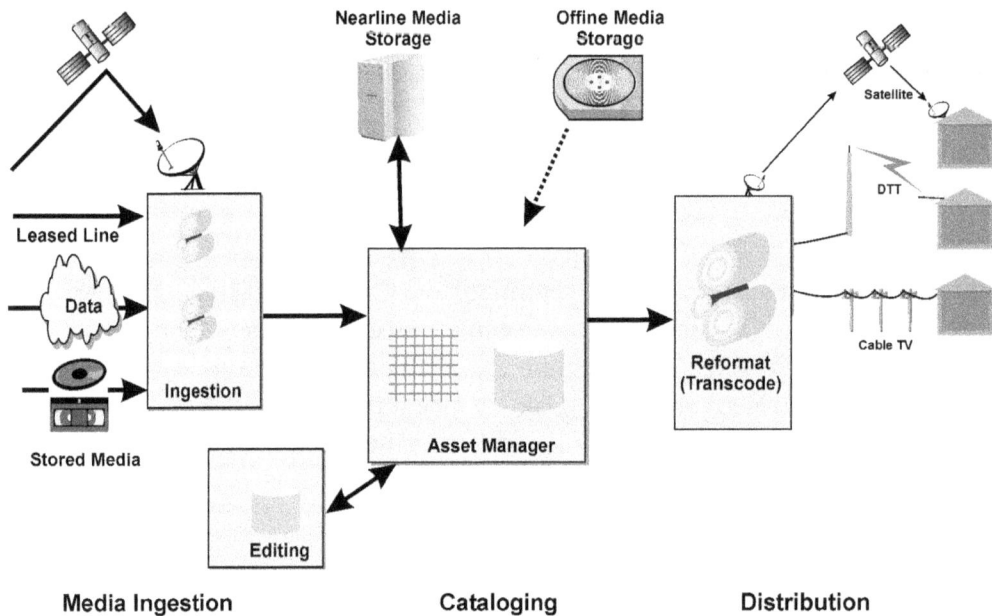

Figure 1.31, TV Asset Storage Systems

Content Processing

Content processing is the adaptation, modification or merging of media into other formats. Content processing may include graphics processing, encoding and/or transcoding.

Graphics Processing

A graphics processor is an information-processing device that is dedicated to the acquisition, analysis and manipulation of graphics images. Graphics processing may be required to integrate (merge or overlay) graphic images with the underlying programs.

Content Encoding

Content encoding is the manipulation (coding) of information or data into another form. Content encoding may include media compression (reducing bandwidth), transmission coding (adapting for the transmission channel) and channel coding (adding control commands for specific channels).

Transcoding

Transcoding is the conversion of digital signals from one coding format to another. An example of transcoding is the conversion of MPEG-2 compressed signals into MPEG-4 AVC coded signals.

Ad Insertion

Ad insertion is the process of inserting an advertising message into a media stream such as a television program. For broadcasting systems, Ad inserts can be controlled by a geographic, demographic, psychographic, or other basis that is determined by the distribution network and optionally by the profile of the viewer.

Ad Splicing

An advertising splicer is a device that selects from two or more media program inputs to produce one media output. Ad splicers receive cueing messages (get ready) and splice commands (switch now) to identify when and which media programs will be spliced.

Cue Tones

Cue tones are signals that are embedded within media or sent along with the media that indicate an action or event is about to happen. Cue tones can be simple event signals or they can contain additional information about the event that is about to occur. An example of a cue tone is a signal in a television program that indicates that a time period for a commercial will occur and how long the time period will last.

Analog cue tone is an audio sequence (such as a DTMF tone) that indicates a time period that will be available ("avail") for the insertion of another media program (e.g. a commercial).

An 'avail' is the time slot within which an advertisement is placed. Avail time periods usually are available in standard lengths of 10, 20, 30 or 40 seconds each. Through the use of addressable advertising, which may provide access to hundreds of thousands of ads with different time lengths, it is possible for many different advertisements, going to different audiences, to share a single avail.

Digital Program Insertion (DPI)

Digital program insertion is the process of splicing media segments or programs together. Because digital media is typically composed of key frames and different pictures that compose a group of pictures (GOP), the splicing of digital media is more complex than the splicing of analog media, which has picture information in each frame, allowing direct frame to frame splicing.

Figure 1.32 shows how an ad insertion system works in a CATV network. This diagram shows that the program media is received and a cue tone indicates the beginning of an advertising spot. When the incoming media is received by the splicer/remultiplexer, it informs the ad server that an advertising media clip is required. The ad server provides this media to the splicer which splices (attaches) each ad to the appropriate media stream. The resulting media stream with the new ad is sent to the viewers in the distribution system.

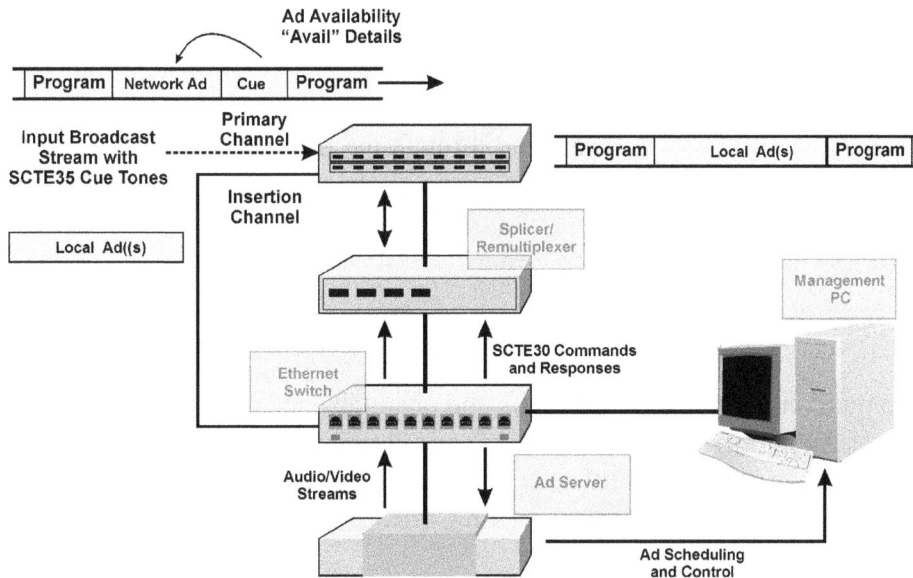

Figure 1.32, Television Ad Splicer

Production Workflow

Production workflow is the sequence of tasks and processes that are necessary to perform projects or assignments.

Workflow Systems

Workflow management systems use work orders to define, setup and manage assets. A work order is a record that contains information that defines and quantifies a process that is used in the production of media (e.g. television programs) or services. The development and management of assets is called workflow.

Distributed Workflow

Distributed workflow is the dividing of processes and systems to allow multiple people or companies to share projects and assignments. Workflow assignments may be allocated and managed through the Internet (cloud workflow) and users may be given access to the portions of projects and assets that they use.

Workflow Automation

As the number of available programs and channels increases, it is desirable to automate the workflow process. Workflow automation is the process of using a system that has established rules or procedures regarding the project assignment, media acquisition, content creation, encoding of media, and scheduling or transmission of content assets.

Distribution Formats

Media may be distributed in a cable TV system in analog and/or digital broadcast video or Internet simulcast.

Broadcast Video Formats

Cable TV system broadcast video formats can include a mix of analog and digital channels. Cable TV system operators are not subject to the analog to digital broadcast conversion requirements that public (wireless) broadcasters have. Each analog TV channel cable TV operators convert to digital can create 6 to 10 digital TV channels.

Internet Simulcasting

Internet simulcasting is the simultaneous sending of a broadcast channel to online video channels. Simulcasting allows a broadcaster to reach viewers in new locations (TV anywhere) who can watch on multiple types of devices including laptops, tablets, smartphones, and other devices.

When sending broadcast channels as Internet TV streams, advertising commercials may be replaced with other commercials. Because the destination of each simulcast stream is known, advertising replacements can be targeted and precisely measured.

Headend

A headend is the master distribution center of a CATV system by which incoming television signals from video sources (e.g., DBS satellites, local studios, video players) are received, amplified, and re-modulated onto TV channels for transmission down the CATV system.

Receivers

The incoming signals for headend systems include satellite receivers, off-air receivers and other types of transmission links. The signals are received (selected) and processed using channel decoders. Headends commonly use integrated receiver devices that combine multiple receiver, decoding and decryption functions into one assembly.

Media Processors

After the headend receives, separates and converts incoming signals into new formats, the signals are selected and encoded so they can be retransmitted (or stored) in the CATV network.

Transmitters

These signals are modulated, amplified and combined so they can be sent on the CATV distribution system.

Figure 1.33 shows a diagram of a simple head-end system. This diagram shows that the head-end gathers programming sources, decodes, selects and retransmits video programming to the distribution network. The video sources to the headend typically include satellite signals, off air receivers, microwave connections and other video feed signals. The video sources are scrambled to prevent unauthorized viewing before being sent to the cable distribution system. The headend receives, decodes and decrypts these channels. This example shows that the programs that will be broadcasted are supplied to encoders and modulators to produce television channels on multiple frequencies. These channels are combined onto a single transmission line by a channel combiner.

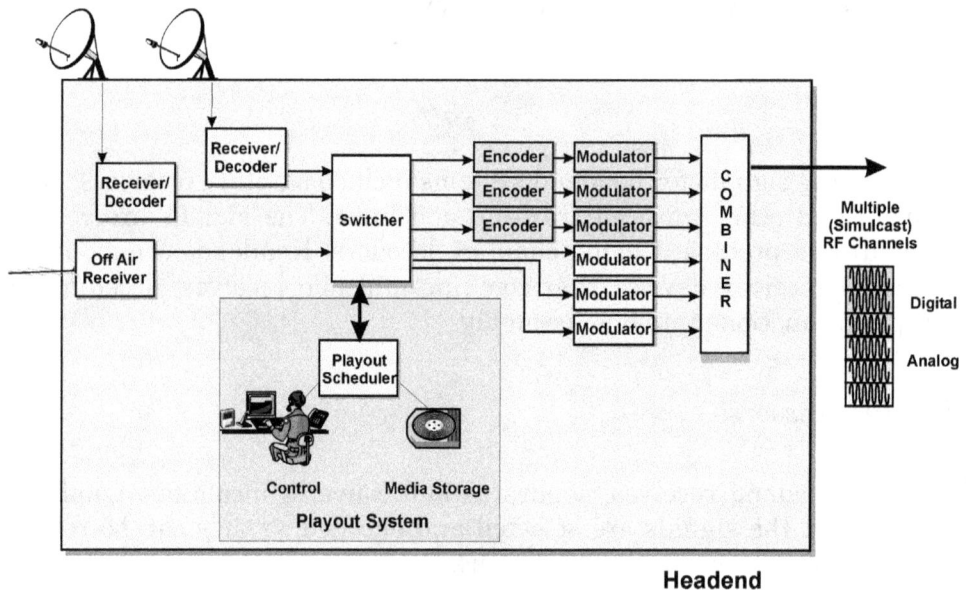

Figure 1.33, Head-end System

A CATV system may be expanded over a large geographic area to include multiple local headend locations. Local headends may be connected to regional headends and regional headends may be connected to a super headend. To reduce the cost of a CATV system, headend systems can be shared by several distribution systems.

Integrated Receiver Decoder (IRD)

An integrated receiver and decoder is a device that can receive, decode, and decrypt broadcast signals (such as from a satellite system) into a form that can be retransmitted on the cable distribution system. In headend systems, IRDs are used to select and process channels from a multi-program transport stream (MPTS) received from a satellite antenna.

The inputs to an IRD (the front end) can include a satellite receiver or a data connection (such as an ATM or IP data connection). The types of processing that an IRD performs can vary from creating analog video signals to creating high definition video digital formats. The outputs of an IRD range from simple video outputs to high-speed IP data connections. Companies that produce IRDs commonly offer variations of IRD (such as analog and digital outputs) that meet the specific needs of the CATV system operator.

Tuner

The IRD has a receiver (tuner) that can select and demodulate a specific RF channel.

Decode

The decoder divides an incoming channel into its component parts.

Decrypt

A decryptor can convert the encrypted information into a form that can be used by the system. Network distribution systems may encrypt program channels so only authorized receivers (paying broadcasters) can decode the content.

Media Processing

IRDs may also change the format (transcode) of the media so that it can be used by other devices.

Figure 1.34 shows the basic function of an integrated receiver device that is used in a cable TV system to receive satellite broadcasted signals and decode the channels. This example shows that an IRD contains a receiver section that can receive and demodulate the MPTS from the satellite. This IRD can decode and decrypt the MPTS to produce several MPEG digital television channels.

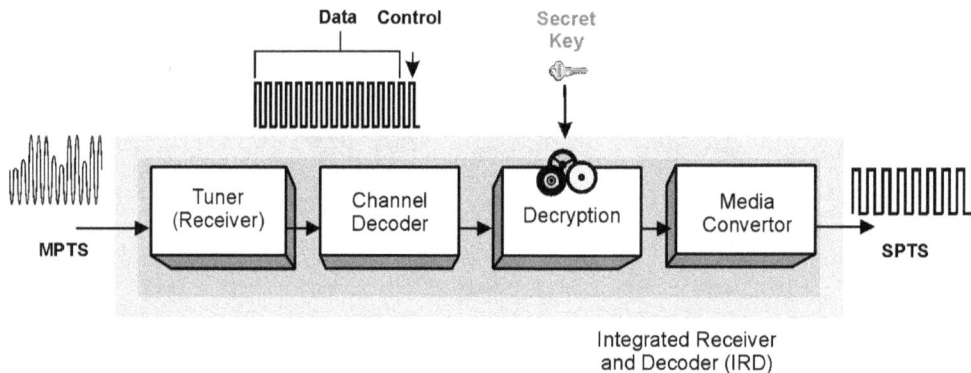

Figure 1.34, Headend Integrated Receiver and Decoder

Off Air Receivers

An off air receiver is a device or assembly that can select, demodulate and decode a broadcasted TV channel. Off air receivers are used in cable television systems to capture local broadcasted channels so they can be re-broadcasted in the local cable television system. Off-air receivers contain a receiver (tuner), demodulator, and a modulator to recreate the off air signal on RF channel that is distributed through the cable TV system.

In some countries (such as the United States), CATV operators are required to rebroadcast local television channels on their cable television systems. These "must carry" regulations are government requirements that dictate that a broadcaster or other media service provider must retransmit (carry) or make available to carry a type of program or content.

Receiver

The off-air receiver contains a tuning head that allows it to select (or be programmed to select) a specific television channel.

Demodulator

Off-air receivers may be simple analog television tuners (e.g. NTSC, PAL or SECAM) or they may be capable of demodulating and decoding digital television channels (e.g. DTT). The demodulated signals may be available as outputs from the off air receiver.

RF Channel Modulator

The RF modulator converts the composite audio and video signal to an RF carrier channel that can be transmitted through the cable TV system.

Figure 1.35 shows a how a cable TV systems uses an off air receiver to retransmit the local TV channel in the cable system. This example shows that a local TV broadcaster is transmitting on channel 5. The cable TV system broadcaster uses the Off-Air receiver convert the broadcast signal to its original video and analog components. The signal is then re-modulated to a channel that can be transmitted on the cable TV system.

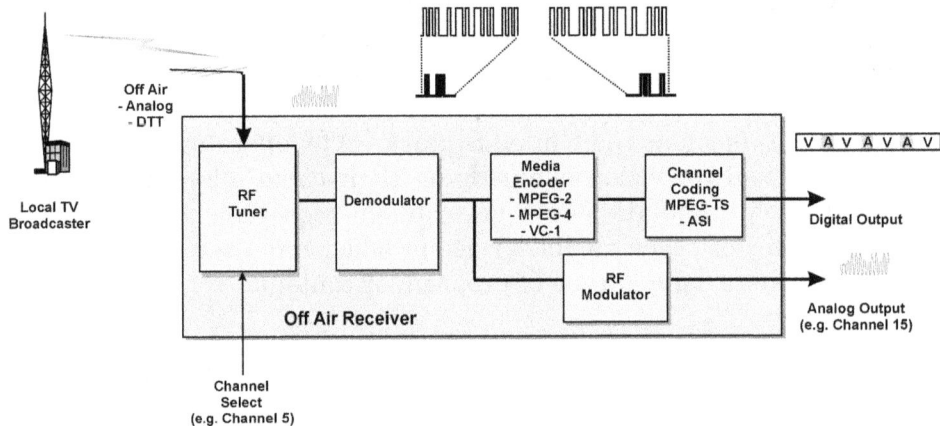

Figure 1.35, Off Air Receiver

Media Encoders

A media encoder is a device that processes one or more input signals (such as a video and audio input) into a specified form for transmission and/or storage (such as a MPEG). Media encoders that are used in television systems receive and process video and audio inputs, compress the media, and format the data for transmission through the network.

Input Formats

TV media encoders receive and process video and audio signals. These signals may be in analog or digital form. If they are in analog form, the signals are converted into a raw (high speed) digital format.

Media Compression

Media encoders contain video and audio compression processes and each encoder may contain multiple types or versions of media encoding (such as MPEG-2 and MPEG-4). The encoder compression function analyzes the video and audio signals and selects an appropriate model that will represent the original signal.

Channel Coding

After the signals are compressed, they are structured in a format that can be transmitted through the network. This includes the transmission channel alternating (time sharing) between video and audio media and adding control signaling information. A common transmission format used in television broadcasting systems is the MPEG transport stream format (MPEG-TS). The MPEG-TS format identifies each media stream (video stream, audio stream), that is part of the program using program identifier (PID) codes.

Figure 1.36 shows a functional diagram of a MPEG media encoder. This example shows that video and audio signals are filtered and digitized by the

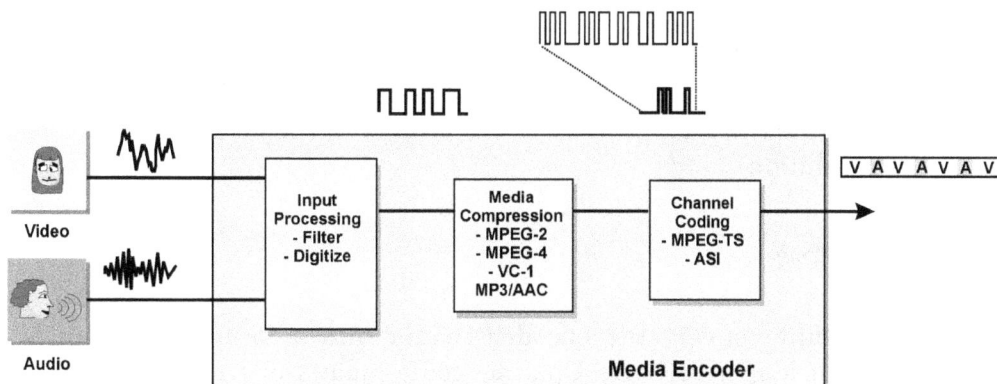

Figure 1.36, MPEG Media Encoder

media encoder. The high-speed digital signals are compressed in by media encoders (MPEG, VC-1, MP3, or AAC). The compressed media signals are then organized into a format that can be transmitted through the network.

Transcoders

A transcoder is a device or assembly that transforms media from one format into another format. Transcoders enable transmission systems that used different types of encoding (such as satellite and cable TV systems) to be interconnected with little or no loss in functionality. A transcoder contains a media decoder, performs media encoding, and may add channel coding to the re-encoded signal.

Media Decoding

A media transcoder contains a media decoder that can receive and convert the incoming media channel into a format that can be used by the media encoder.

Media Encoding

The media encoder section of a transcoder may compress and encode the media into another format (such as converting from MPEG-2 to MPEG-4). The media encoder may also change other media characteristics such as its transmission rate (rate adaptation) or the profiles of the media (such as lowering the resolution).

Channel Coding

Transcoders may convert the encoded media into a format that can be broadcasted such as MPEG-TS. Channel coding may involve converting the digital media from variable packet sizes to fixed length packets and interleaving audio and video media.

Figure 1.37 shows how transcoding can be used to convert media formats. This example shows a media transcoder decodes and re-encodes media into a different format. The decoder converts incoming media into a form that it can use to re-encode into another form. This transcoder can convert media into MPEG-2, MPEG-4 or VC-1 media formats.

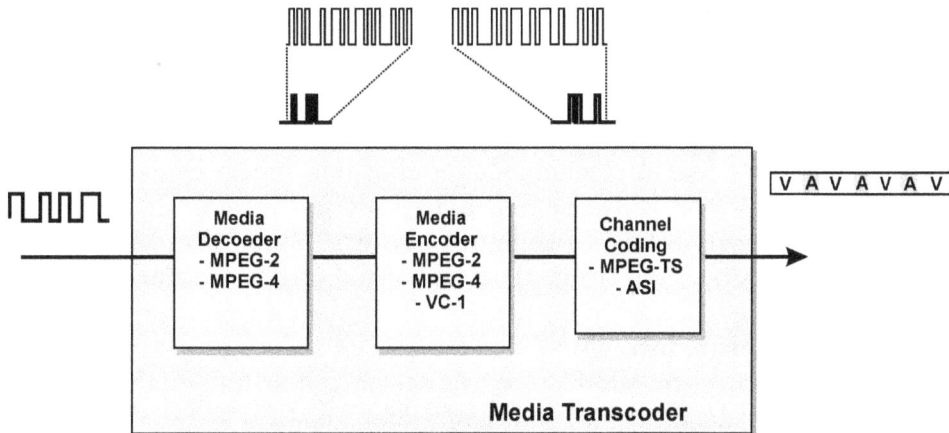

Figure 1.37, TV Transcoder

Rate Shaper

Rate shapers are devices or assemblies in a communication system that adapt and/or transform the transmission rate of channels or media streams one system to the transmission rate of another system.

Rate shapers can be used to adjust the transmission rates from a signal source (such as from a broadcast distribution system) to the transmission rates that are required by the distribution system (such as a cable TV or mobile video broadcast system). Video data rates can vary based on the content they carry. Rapidly changing scenes require higher data rates. Rate shapers can adapt the data rate (temporarily lowering the resolution) to multiple channels can fit into a single RF transmission channel.

Variable Bit Rate (VBR)

A variable bit rate feed is a media source that has a data transmission rate that varies over time (such as digital video). Video channels can be setup to have a varying bit rates when rapid content changes occurs or additional data is sent on the channel.

Constant Bit Rate (CBR)

A constant bit rate feed is a media source that has a data transmission rate that does not vary over time (such as a digital transmission channel). Video channels can be set to have a constant bit rate. When there are multiple video channels on a single transmission channel (MPTS), different constant bit rates can be set for each channel. For example, a program that has relatively few changes (a documentary about the sky) may be given a low data rate while a program that has many changes (such as a football game) may be given a higher data rate (action scenes look good).

Bit Rate Adjustment

Bit rate adjustment is the modification of data compression so the combined transmission rates for multiple channels that have variable bandwidth rates so they can operate over transmission channels that have constant or limited maximum transmission bit rates.

Figure 1.38 shows how a rate shaper can combine multiple digital television channels to help adjust the maximum bandwidth usage. This example shows 3 digital television channels that have variable bandwidth due to high video activity periods (action scenes with high motion). The combined data rate is shown at the bottom. The combined data rate has a peak data rate that is larger than the 30 Mbps transmission channel can allow. As a result, one or more of the input MPEG channels must use a higher compression rate (temporary lower picture quality).

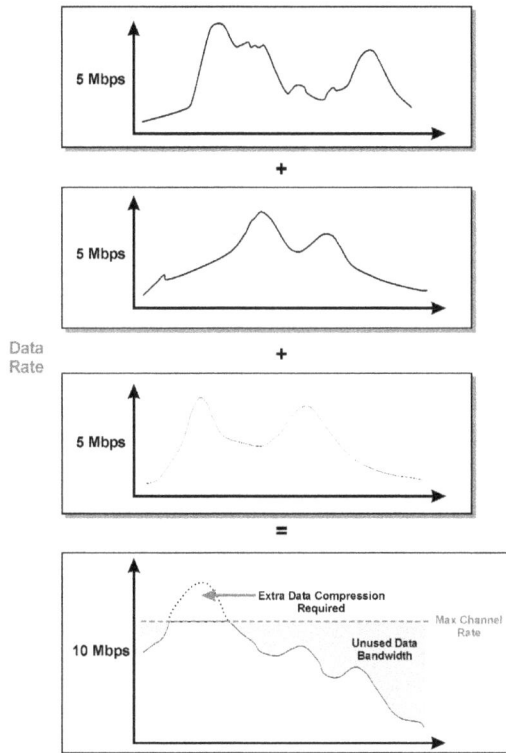

Figure 1.38, MPEG Statistical Multiplexing

Channel Modulators

A channel modulator is used to convert video and audio signals into RF television broadcast channels. Channel modulators are used in cable-TV networks to convert a video program signal (analog or digital) into a RF carrier frequency for a television channel that is distributed through the CATV network. The modulator converts both video and audio signals. The frequency of this channel modulator carrier determines the television channel number (e.g., 2 to 120) that the program will be received on by subscribers.

Video Input

Video input may be in analog form or digital form.

Audio Input

Analog input may be in analog form or digital form.

Transport Streams

MPEG transport streams (MPEG-TS) use a fixed length packet size and a packet identifier locates each transport packet within the transport stream. A packet identifier in an MPEG system identifies the packetized elementary streams (PES) of a program channel. A program (such as a television show) is usually composed of multiple PES channels (e.g. video and audio). Cable television systems commonly use an MPEG transport stream (MPEG-TS) to transfer multiple programs on each RF transmission channel.

RF Output

Channel modulators convert analog or digital channels modulated RF signals. Each RF channel may contain one (analog) or multiple (digital) program channels. A cable TV system can have up to 125 RF channels on its broadcast system. Each channel modulator can be set to a RF channel frequency (54-806 MHz).

Figure 1.39 shows how channel modulators convert video and audio signals into an RF signal. The video and audio signals are combined to a composite video signal. This is provided to a mixer which shifts the composite video signal to the RF channel frequency. This channel modulator allows the user to adjust the frequency of the RF channel (channel selector switch).

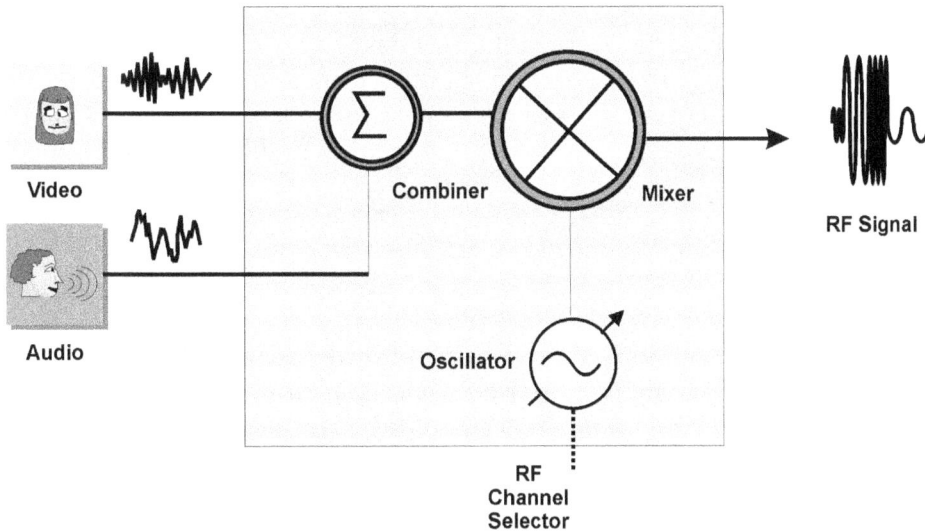

Figure 1.39, TV Channel Modulator

Channel Processors

A channel processor is a device or assembly that can receive, modify, and produce a new RF channel signal. A common CATV television channel processing function is to change the frequency of the channel signal so that a channel that is received on one frequency can be shifted (translated) to another frequency that is sent on a transmission system.

Receiver

The receiver uses a tuner to select (separate) the transmission channel from the incoming signal (an RF channel). This includes a demodulator that can capture the information signal from the carrier. For digital signals, a channel decoder is used to identify specific sections of the digital transmission channel that will be used for the selected TV channel.

Media Processor

A media process is used to convert the received signal into video and audio formats. The channel processor may make video and audio level adjustments and correct for time delays necessary for video and audio synchronization. The compression of digital video and audio coding commonly results in different amounts of time shifting.

RF Modulator

The adjusted media signal is then converted into a form that can be transferred (transmitted) to the distribution system. This may be in RF, optical, or digital formats. For RF channels, the digital signals modulate the RF carrier signal.

Figure 1.40 shows how channel processors can receiver, process, and produce new TV channels. The channel processor contains a tuner that can select a specific RF channel from an incoming broadcast line. The demodulator recovers the video and audio signals from the selected channel and may perform processing (such as audio level adjustment). The video and

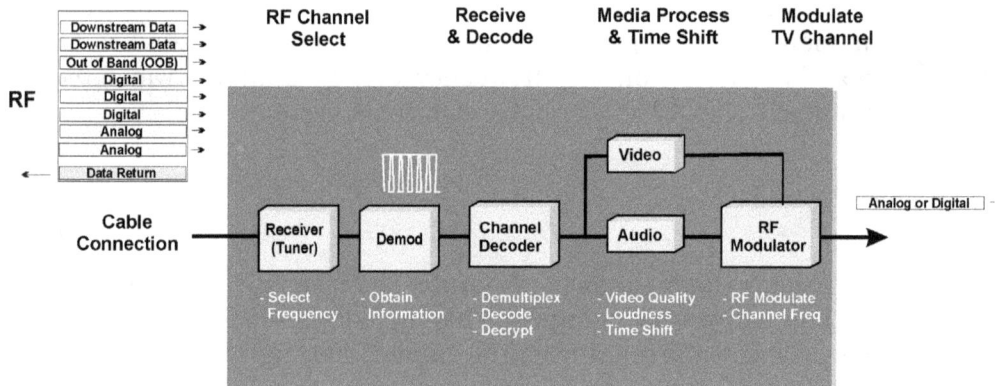

Figure 1.40, TV Channel Processors

audio signal is provided to a modulator and the channel processor produces are RF carrier signal output on a desired channel.

Channel Signal Combiners

Channel combiners are devices or filter assemblies that allows several modulated carrier signals (physical channels) to be grouped on to the same transmission channel (distribution system).

RF Channel Coupling

Each transmission (transport) channel operates on a separate frequency band. CATV systems may allow up to 125 RF channels on a single transmission channel. Because each transport channel can carry multiple logical channels (typically 4 to 6 TV channels per carrier), a digital cable television system can provide hundreds of television channels.

RF Channel Isolation

Channel combiners allow multiple RF channels to connect to the same transmission line. To keep signals from the transmitter of one RF channel from being received and interfering with RF transmitters of other transmission channels, the channel combiner provides some port to port isolation (attenuation between the ports).

Passive and Active Combiners

The types of combiner networks include active and passive combiners. Active combiners include amplifiers to increase the signal level as it passes through the combining network. Passive combiners use filters to isolate the signals from each other.

Figure 1.41 shows how CATV channel combiners are used to combine different RF channel signals into a common transmission line. This diagram shows a passive CATV channel combiner that is composed of multiple signal couplers. Each coupler (tap) allows signals to pass through to the transmission line while providing some isolation (signal attenuation) from other transmitters.

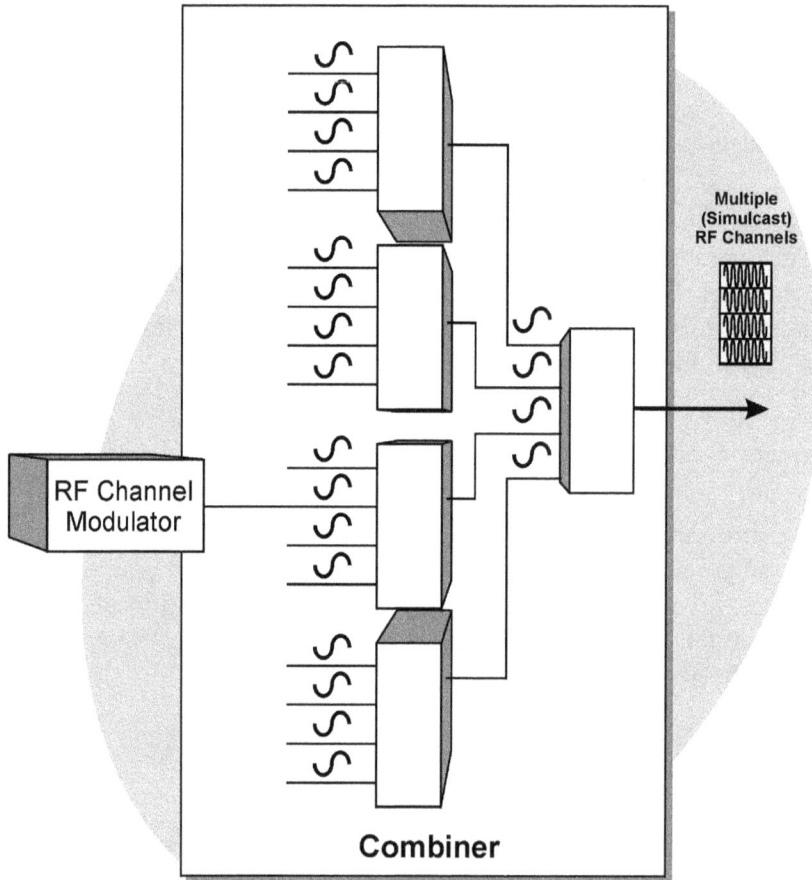

Figure 1.41, CATV Channel Combiners

Distribution Network

The distribution network is the part of a cable television system that connects the head-end of the system (video and media sources) to the customer's equipment. A distribution network is composed of a core network, access network, and home media network.

Core Network

The core network is the central network portion of a communication system which primarily provides interconnection and transfer between the headend and between edge access networks. Core networks in CATV systems are commonly setup as fiber rings and spurs. A fiber ring is an optical network of network topology with a connection that provides a complete loop. The ring topology is used to provide a backup distribution path as traffic to be quickly rerouted in the other direction around the loop in the event of a fiber cut. A fiber spur is a fiber line that extends the fiber ring into another area for final distribution.

Hybrid Fiber Coax (HFC)

CATV systems commonly use a mix of fiber rings in the core and coax lines (hybrid fiber and coax) to connect the customer. The hybrid fiber coax (HFC) system provides high-speed backbone data interconnection lines (the fiber portion) to interconnect end user video and data equipment. HFC systems convert (shift) the RF channels at the head end into optical signals that can travel down a fiber. When the optical signal reaches a fiber node, it is converted (downshifted) back onto the radio frequency band which then travels down the coaxial line.

Video Distribution Servers

A CATV system may include multiple video distribution servers located at multiple points in their network which temporarily store movies and content. This provides more capacity for video on demand services (number of active users per video server) and reduces the distance and number of connection paths required for video in demand users (available distribution connection channels).

Automatic Redundancy

CATV networks are typically designed to automatically redirect transmissions paths to enable the system to continue to operate when failures occur. This can be done with network reconfiguration and backup (spare) equipment. For example, the core network may be designed as a dual ring where the same TV signals circle around the network. When the loop is cut, the signal is automatically redirected at the cut point so the signal can reach the disconnected part of the network using the other loop.

Figure 1.42 shows a typical cable distribution system that uses a combination of fiber optic cable for the core distribution and coaxial cable for the local connection. This diagram shows that the multiple RF television channels at the head-end of the cable television system are shifted in frequency to allow distribution through high-speed fiber cable. The fiber cable is connected in a loop around the cable television service area so that if a break in the cable occurs, the signal will automatically be available from the other parts of the loop. The loop is connected (tapped) at regular points by a fiber hub that can distribute the optical signals on fiber spurs. The fiber spurs end at fiber nodes that convert the optical signals into RF television signals that are distributed on the local coaxial cable network.

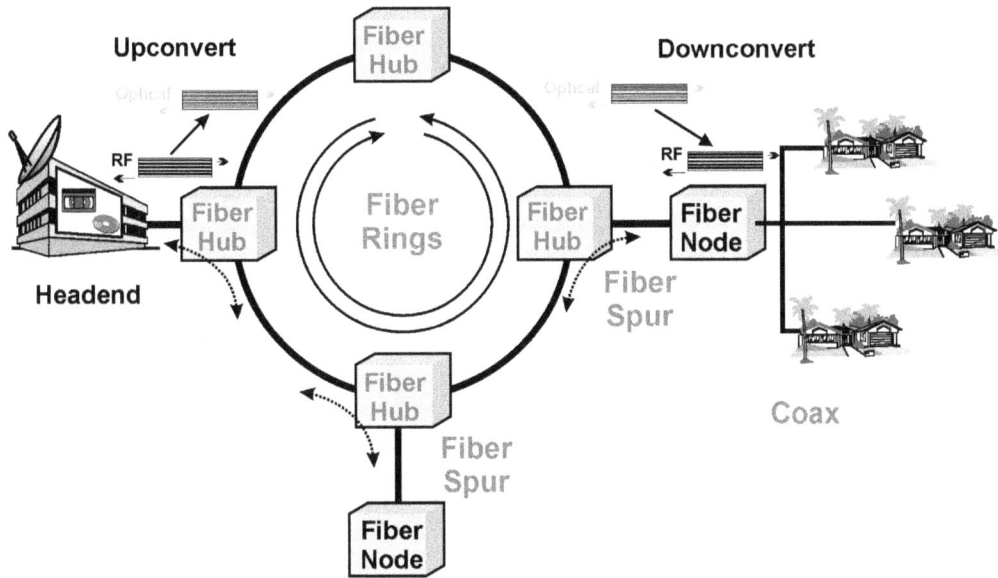

Figure 1.42, Hybrid Cable Television Distribution Network

Access Network

An access network is the portion of a communication network that allows individual subscribers or devices to connect to the core network. The CATV system access network allows the end user device (e.g. set top box) communicate with the system. Traditionally, CATV access networks have been coaxial lines with multiple RF channels. However, CATV systems have started to provide television services through other networks such as the Internet or Wireless systems.

For coax CATV access networks, there are several types of RF channels. These include analog TV channels (generally being phased out), digital TV channels, data channels, and out of band control channels.

Access Node Transmission Conversion

The core network connect to the access networks by nodes which select optical channels and converts them to RF signals that are sent into the homes. The access nodes (typically optical network units (ONU) contain channel modulators and RF amplifiers.

Access Channel Types

Access RF channels may include a mix of analog, digital, and control channels.

Analog RF channels transfer television programming in analog form (e.g. NTSC or PAL). These signals may be available for anyone to use, or they may be scrambled so the receiver must decode (descramble) the analog program.

Digital channels transfer television programming in digital form (e.g. MPEG). The programs transferred by digital channels are usually compressed so each digital RF channel carries multiple television programs. Digital channels may be available for anyone to use or they may be encrypted so the receiver must decode (decrypt) the digital program.

Cable systems send (and optionally receive) control information to the devices, such as channel identification information and programming guides. The control messages may be sent on the television channel that is displaying the program (in band) or on separate control channels (out of band). When the data is sent in band, the control data shares the bandwidth with the television programming. When the data is sent on out of band channels, it is sent on other RF channels.

Data RF channels are designed to efficiently transfer user data (such as Internet data) between users and the cable system. Data RF channels can use a very efficient form of modulation (such as QAM) from the system to the end user, allowing the cable system to provide high speed data from the system to the receiver (up to 30 Mbps to 40 Mbps) per RF channel. Because signals from multiple users are combined when they are sending data to the cable system, this increases the amount of noise level so a more robust (less efficient) modulation form is used (such as QPSK), which can provide medium speed data from the users to the system (up to 2 to 5 Mbps per RF channel). Data channels are defined in the DOCSIS specification available from CableLabs.

Channel Access Data Carousel

System broadcast channel information is typically repeated in carousel form so that receivers can capture and store the information when it becomes available. If the receiver cannot obtain the entire data block of information, it can simply wait until the next transmission of data. Each unique block of information is assigned an identification code to allow the receiver to determine if it has already received the block or if it is a new block of information it needs to decode and store.

Because data channels can transfer information much faster than the older out of band (OOB) channels, when data channels are available to send the system information, the out of band channels do not need to be used. However, systems that upgrade to data channels may continue to use the OOB channels, as the existing customer equipment may not have data channel capability.

Gateways

Gateways are an access device (typically a modem) that allows a service provider (such as Cable TV or DSL) to monitor and potentially configure and control devices on the other side of the gateway (e.g. a Home Network). Some service providers offer a service for home network management. It can be helpful to be able to identify equipment and configuration problems in a home network that can effect the viewing experience quality.

Figure 1.43 shows how the access portion of a CATV uses RF channels to communicate with a set top box. This example shows a CATV network that has a mix of analog TV, digital TV, control channels and data communication channels. System information may be repeatedly sent using in band, out of band or data channels. This example shows that the CATV system may communicate with older set top boxes (STBs) that only have one tuner or it may be communicating with set top boxes that have multiple tuners. The STBs with multiple tuners can simultaneously receive programs and system information, which allows the viewer to continue to watch their programs without interruption.

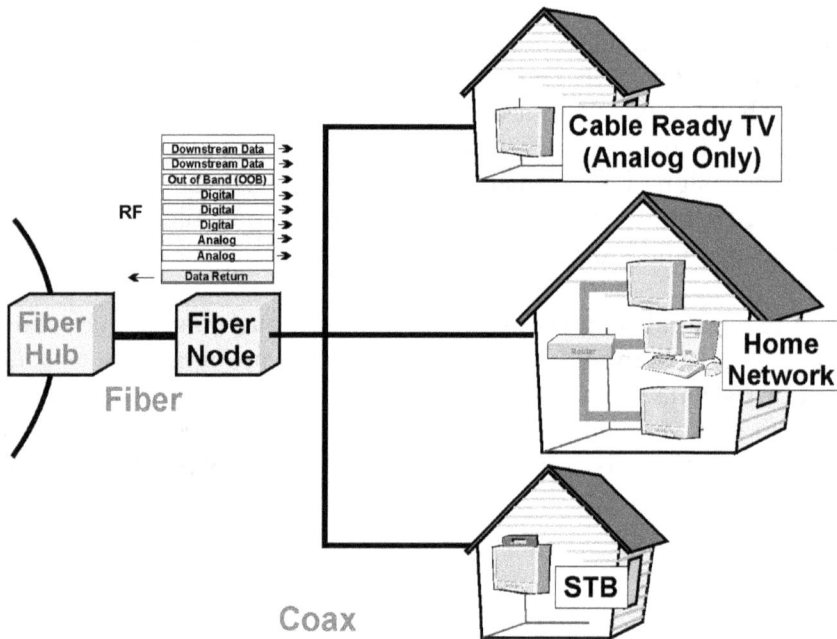

Figure 1.43, Cable Television Access Network

Home Network

A home media network is the equipment and software that is used to transfer media and data in a customer's premises, home or personal area. A home network may be used to connect TVs, terminals (computers) to the cable TV system and other networks. Some common types of home networks include wired local area network (data cable), wireless local area networks (WLAN), electrical powerline data, coaxial (CATV and other signals), optical, and phoneline data.

While CATV system operators may not own home network equipment, it can be important to understand what home network equipment the customer uses because it can effect or interfere with CATV services. Home networks may be used to transfer CATV RF signals (such as on Coax) or be used to provide streaming video services (over data connections.)

Home networks are evolving to detect the types of media they are transferring. By understanding the type of media (data files -vs- video streams), priorities can be set to ensure a better user experience.

Home network industry standards are evolving and merging enabling multiple types of networks to co-exist in the home. The core industry standard is Ethernet data which allows network devices to easily connect with each other.

Wired LAN

Wired LAN systems use cables to connect routers and communication devices. These cables can be composed of twisted pairs of wires or other types of cable. Wired LAN data transmission rates vary from 10 Mbps to more than 10 Gbps. While wired Ethernet systems offer high data throughput and reliability, many homes do not have dedicated wiring installed for Ethernet LAN networks and for the homes that do have data networks, the data outlets are often located near computers rather than near televisions.

When wired LAN systems use twisted wire pairs in the cable, the maximum data transmission rate (cable rating) is influenced by the number of twists in the cable wire pairs. Cable wire pairs that have a higher the number of twists can send data at a higher transmission rate.

A data cable that is used for wired LAN networks are classified by the amount of data it can carry in by the Electronics Industry Association/Telecommunications Industry Association EIA/TIA 586 cabling standard. In general, category 1 rated cable is unshielded twisted-pair (UTP) telephone cable (not suitable for high-speed data transmissions). Category 2 cable is UTP cable that can be used for transmission speed up to 4 Mbps. Category 3 UTP cable can be used at data transmission speeds of 10 Mbps. Category 4 UTP cable can transmit up to 16Mbps and is commonly used for Token Ring networks. Category 5 cable is rated for data transmission speeds up to 100 Mbps. Category 5E (enhanced) has the same frequency range as Category 5 with a lower amount of signal transfer (crosstalk) so it can be used for 1 Gbps Ethernet systems. Category 6 cable has a frequency rating of 250 MHz and 10 Gbps transmission has been demonstrated.

Wired home LAN systems are typically installed as a star network. The star point (the center of thee network) is usually a router or hub that is located near a broadband modem. LAN wiring is not a commonly installed in many homes and when LAN wiring is installed, LAN connection outlets are unlikely to be located near television viewing points.

Wireless Local Area Network (WLAN)

Wireless local area network (WLAN) systems allow computers and workstations to communicate with each other using radio propagation as the transmission medium. The wireless LAN can be connected to an existing wired LAN as an extension, or it can form the basis of a new network. Wi-Fi television distribution is important because it is an easy and efficient way to get digital multimedia information where it is needed without the addition of new wires.

Wireless transmission systems operate within defined frequency bands, have varying data transmission rates, and may include multibeam transmission capability.

Frequency Bands

Frequency bands are the range of frequencies that are used or allocated for radio services. The frequency bands that are commonly used for home media networks are in the unlicensed industrial, scientific, and medical (ISM) band. These bands of the electromagnetic spectrum include frequency ranges at 902-928 MHz, 2.4-2.484 GHz, and 5.725-5.825 GHz frequency bands which do not require an operator's license. Most wireless LAN devices operate in the 2.4 GHz and 5.7 GHz band.

The requirements for unlicensed frequency bands (maximum power levels and transmission times) were designed to allow multiple devices to co-exist with each other with varying levels of interference. In general, there tend to be more devices that operate in the 2.4 GHz region than in the 5.7 GHz region which means that interference may be higher in the 2.4 GHz band. It is possible to setup home networks to use 2.4 GHz wireless LANs for data transmission and 5.7 GHz wireless LANs for video distribution.

Data Transfer Rates

The data transfer rates that are available on wireless LANs very based on modulation types, interference levels, and channel bonding. Wireless LAN data transmission rates vary from 2 Mbps to over 54 Mbps. Higher data transmission rates (up to 300 Mbps) are possible through the use of channel bonding (combining channels). In the mid 2000s, several new WLAN standards were created to enable and ensure different types of quality of service (QoS) over WLAN.

Multimedia signals such as television and music are converted into WLAN (Ethernet) packet data format and distributed through the home or business by wireless signals. Some versions of the 802.11 WLAN specifications include the ability to apply a quality of service (QoS) to the distributed signals giving priority to ensure that time sensitive information (such as video and audio) can get through and non-time sensitive information (such as web browsing).

Power Line Communication (PLC)

Electrical powerline communication (PLC) networks send data signals along electrical power lines. PLC systems have transitioned from low speed data, simple command and control systems (light controls) to high-speed multimedia networks, along with the ability to transfer a variety of media types that have different transmission and management requirements. Each of the applications that operate through a PLC system can have different communication requirements that typically include a maximum data transmission rate, continuous or bursty transmission, packet delay and jitter and error tolerance. The PLC system may manage these connections using a mix of protocols that can define and manage quality of service (QoS). There are multiple PLC system types including HomePlug and HomeGrid (g.hn).

Electrical power line carrier is a signal that can be transmitted over electrical power lines. A power line carrier signal is transmitted above the standard 50 Hz or 60 Hz power line power frequency. Power line communication systems have evolved to overcome transmission challenges that include electrical noise, phase coupling, and changing connection paths (topology).

The power line communication systems developed in the 1970s used relatively low frequencies such as 450 kHz to transfer data on power lines. The amount of data that could be transferred was limited and the applications typically consisted of controlling devices such as light switches and outlets. Some of the early home automation systems include: X-10, CeBus and LONworks.

Electrical Noise

Electrical power lines commonly are exposed to undesired electrical noise signals that are created from a variety of sources such as brush motors, halogen lamps, dimmer switches, and devices that produce noise signals that travel into the electrical lines. Electrical noise signals can be random and have can cause the lost of data packets. Home media networks that use electrical power lines can use processes to detect and isolate much of the electrical noise signals.

Phase Coupling

Older (legacy) power line communication systems had challenges with wiring systems that used two or more phases of electrical power. The signals that traveled on wires for one phase of the electrical system would need to travel through other devices (such as 220 volt appliances) to reach wires that were connected to the other phase of electric.

Newer power line communication systems use higher frequency signals that can travel directly across (jump across) wires in an electrical panel so the entire home can distribute the home media network signals.

Changing Topology

The connection paths within an electrical distribution system can change over time. Connection paths may change when light switches are turned on (connected) or off (opened) and when appliances cycle on and off. These new connection paths may result in signal reflections that can cause distortion. Home media networks may be able to detect and rapidly adapt to the changing topology conditional of electrical wiring within homes.

Although power line communication systems could technically transfer data in the 1970s and 1980s, improvements in the power line data transfer rates necessary for home data networking did not occur until the early 2000s.

Part of the motivation to make advances in power line communication was the increased need for home networking.

Power line premises distribution for home media is important because televisions, set-top boxes, digital media adapters (DMAs) and other media devices are already connected to power outlets already installed in a home or small businesses. These lines can be used to transmit rich multimedia content where it is desired.

HomePlug

HomePlug is a PLC system specification that defines the signals and operation for data and entertainment services that can be provided through electric power lines. The HomePlug specification has evolved from low bandwidth data services to advanced audio/visual disribution. Development of the HomePlug specification is overseen by the HomePlug® Powerline Alliance. More information about Homeplug can be found at www.Homeplug.org.

HomeGrid

HomeGrid is a multimedia home networking forum that helps to develop and promote the G.hn industry specification for different types of media that can be sent over different types of transmission lines (copper, power, telephone). The G.hn specification enables data transmission rates up to 1 Gbps [14].More information about HomeGrid can be found at www.homegridforum.org/

Coaxial

Coaxial cable premises distribution systems transfer user information over coaxial television lines in a home or building. Coaxial distribution systems may simply distribute (split) the signal to other televisions in the home, or they may be more sophisticated home data networks.

When coaxial systems are setup as data networks, data signals at high frequencies (above 860 MHz) are combined with broadcast signals over the same coaxial lines. Coaxial cable data transmission rates vary from 1 Mbps to over 1 Gbps and many homes have existing cable television networks and outlets, which are located near video accessory and television viewing points.

Multimedia over Coax Alliance (MoCA)

Multimedia over Coax Alliance is a non-profit association that works to help develop and promote unified information about networking technologies, products and services that are primarily distributed over coax cabling systems within a building or premises. The MoCA system uses higher frequency RF channels (not CATV channels) to send very high-speed data transfer (1 Gbps+) with almost no signal interference or leakage. More information about MoCA can be found at www.mocalliance.org/

Tree Distribution

Coaxial systems are commonly setup as a tree distribution system. The root of the tree is usually at the entrance point to the home or building. The tree may divide several times as it progresses from the root to each television outlet through the use of signal splitters.

Each time the signal passes through a splitter, the energy is divided between each of the connection paths (ports on the splitter). A splitter that has 4 ports will have at least 75% reduction in signal power that goes to each port.

Tree distribution can become a challenge in homes that have many cable connections. To overcome some of the loss in a cable distribution system, RF amplifiers can be used. The amplifiers typically need to be two-way amplifiers so they can carry data signals back to the CATV system.

Cable Television Co-Existence

Home media networks that operate on coaxial lines may need to co-exist with existing television systems existing TV signals. This can be accomplish by transmitting the home media network signals on frequencies that are above the frequency range of the other television signals (typically above 850 MHz). This allows for the simultaneous distribution of existing TV signals (such as cable television channels) and home media network signals.

Coaxial Wire Types

There are different types of coaxial cable and their key characteristics include frequency range and attenuation level. Older coaxial cable types (such as RG-59) tend to have a lower frequency range and higher attenuation level than newer types of cable (such as RG-62). In general, as the frequency of signal increases, the amount of attenuation also increases. Home media networks that use coaxial lines can adapt to this by sensing the signal attenuation levels at the receiving devices and increasing their transmitter power levels for higher frequencies.

Because the coax cable is shielded and RF channels are virtually free from the effects of interfering signals, coaxial cable provides a large information pipe that is capable of distributing multiple wide radio frequency channels. Coax is already installed in many homes, and television outlets are commonly located near media equipment such as televisions, VCRs and cable modems. Coaxial cable is easy to install and expand.

Telephone Line

Home media networks may transfer user information over existing telephone lines in a home or building. Home media networks that use telephone lines can have data transmission rates that range from 1 Mbps to over 300 Mbps. Telephone line outlets may be located near television viewing points making it easy to connect adapters or viewing devices that have telephone line home media network connections.

Telephone line home data network specifications was developed by the home phoneline networking alliance. In 2013, the HomePNA association merged into the HomeGrid forum. For more information, visit www.homegridforum.org.

Wire Types

Telephone lines to and from the telephone company may contain analog voice signals, uplink data signals, and downlink data signals. These frequency bands typically range up to 1 MHz (some DSL systems go up to 12 MHz). Home media networks that use telephone lines may use frequencies above the 1 MHz frequency band to transfer signals to telephone jacks throughout the house so they do not interfere with existing telephone signals.

Adapter boxes or integrated communication circuits convert the video and/or data signals to high frequency channels that are distributed to different devices located throughout the house. To ensure the phone line signals do not transfer out of the home to other nearby homes, a blocking filter may be installed on the line that enters into the home.

The earliest telephone line home multimedia communication systems were used to allow computers to transfer files with each other (home data network) and to connect data communication accessories such as printers. These early telephone line data communication systems sent a limited amount of data using frequencies slightly above the audio frequency band. These early systems had relatively low data transmission rates and they were fairly limited when compared to automatic telephone line communication systems.

As home media network signals travel down telephone lines, a portion of the signal is lost through the wires (absorbed or radiated). Signal frequency, the type of wire, how the wire is installed and the length of the wire are key factors in determining the amount of energy that is lost. Generally, as the length of a telephone increases and the number of outlets increases, the amount of attenuation also increases.

Interfering Signals

A challenge for transmitting data over the phone line is the presence of interfering signals and the variability of the characteristics of the telephone lines. Interference signals include telephone signals (ringing, DTMF, modems) and signals from outside source (such as AM radio stations). Home media networks that operate on telephone lines may be designed to detect and avoid these signals by selecting sub-channels that do not have significant interference levels.

Splices

Phone line data communication systems need to work through existing telephone lines (which may be unshielded) that are connected with each other in a variety of ways (e.g. looped or spliced throughout a house) and may have a variety of telephone devices and accessories attached to it. Variability can be caused by poor installation of telephone wiring, telephone cords and changes in the characteristics of the telephone devices and accessories. To overcome the effects of interference and the variability of transmission lines, home media network systems can adaptive transmission processes.

Signal Leakage

Because some of the energy leaks out of the telephone line, the maximum signal level authorized by regulatory authorities (such as the Federal Communication Commission) is relatively low. Home media networks may reduce the transmitter power level to the minimum levels necessary for devices in the system to receive a signal (power level control) which reduces the amount of signal leakage.

Home Optical Networks

Some home networks (or portions of them) may transfer data over fibers in optical cables. The transmission rate in some optical can dramatically vary based on the type of fiber and the type of optical signal source such as laser (very high) or LED (moderately high). The choices of fiber and optical transmitter can also determine the types of connectors and installation that may be required for optical systems. Typical data transmission rates for home optical networks ranges from 25 Mbps to over 400 Mbps.

Fiber Type

Optical fibers can be designed and produced to transfer light in different ways. Single mode fibers transfer a single wavelength (color) of light through a very precise inner core (smaller than the size of a human hair). Multiple mode fibers can transfer multiple wavelengths of light through a much wider inner core. Because multimode fibers allow the light to bounce around within the core, the light pulses tend to become less precise (more fuzzy) which limits the maximum data transmission rate and distance that can be used. However, the installation of multimode fibers with very large optical cores allows for bending of the fiber (such as around corners) which cannot be done with single mode fibers.

Optical Type

The transmitter for optical systems can use light amplification for the stimulation of radiation (LASER) or light emitting diodes (LED). Lasers create highly focused signals which can transfer data at very high speeds (10 Gbps+). LEDs tend create light signals that are more disbursed (less focused). The light energy from Lasers may be enough to cause harm to people, especially in the eyes. Home media networks that use optical lines may use LEDs instead of Lasers to ensure the system is safe to install and use.

Connection Type

Traditional optical connectors require precise connection points (cutting and polishing) to avoid optical signal reflections and distortion. For low cost plastic passive optical fiber (POF) that have relatively wide cores, simple cutters can be used. The POF fibers can be pushed into a spring loaded optical connector with no polishing required.

Figure 1.44 shows the types of home networks. Wired LAN is a universal packet data standard that works with wired connection and on top of other systems. Wireless LAN (WLAN) 802.11 operates on multiple frequencies and is evolving to focused beam transmission for higher data rates and lower interference. Powerline data (HomePlug and HomeGrid) transfers

Network Type	Key Standards	Key Features
Wired LAN	Ethernet, IEEE 802.3	Universal packet data standard that works on wires and on top of other systems.
Wireless LAN (WiFI)	IEEE 802.11	Multiple frequencies, evolving to focused beam transmission for higher data rates and lower interference.
Powerline Data	HomePlug, HomeGrid	Transfers data through electrical power connection which most devices use. Moving to higher transmission frequencies which makes connections more reliable.
Coaxial	MoCA, HomeGrid	Uses higher frequency RF channels (not CATV channels) to send very high-speed data transfer (1 Gbps+) with almost no signal interference or leakage.
Optical Local Area Networks (OLAN)		Passive optical fiber uses LEDs - safe, no interference, and plastic fiber is very flexible.
Phoneline Data	HomeGrid (merged with HomePNA)	Uses inexpensive twisted pair phone lines.

Figure 1.44, Home Network Types

data through electrical power connection and is using higher transmission frequencies to makes connections more reliable. Coax home systems use higher frequency RF channels (not CATV RF channels) to send very high-speed data transfer (1 Gbps+) with almost no signal interference or leakage. Passive optical fiber uses LED for transmission (safe) which has no interference and plastic fiber is very flexible. Phoneline data networks can use inexpensive twisted pair phone lines to send data.

CATV Access Devices

CATV access devices (also called customer premises equipment - CPE) is an electronic unit that receives a transmitted signal and makes it perceptible to a human user or converts it into some other useful form. CATV access devices include set top boxes, cable ready televisions, cable modems and cable telephones. According to the FCC 2017 video competition report, almost all setup top boxes are leased by subscribers in the United States [15].

Viewing Device Functions

Cable television viewing devices adapt RF channels on a cable connection to a format that is accessible by the end user. The key functions for end user devices include interfacing to the cable network, selecting and decoding channels, processing the media into a form usable by humans and providing controls that allow the user to interact with the device.

The network interface for cable television end user devices allows it to receive analog broadcast, digital broadcast, digital control and data channels. The device must select the appropriate RF channel and separate out the component parts of the television signal (video, audio and data). The underlying media is then decoded and decrypted (unscrambled). The media is then converted (rendered) into a form that can be displayed or heard by the end user. A program guide and menu system is provided to allow the user to navigate and select features and services.

Figure 1.45 shows the basic functions of a cable television end user viewing device. This diagram shows that the end user device has a network interface, signal processing, decoding, rendering and user interface. The network interface may contain one or several RF tuners to receive and decode broadcast and control channels. The signal processing receives, selects and demultiplexes the incoming channels. After the channels are received, the channel may require decoding (decryption) for scrambled channels. The STB then converts the data into signals that can be displayed to the viewer (rendering). The STB has a user interface, which allows the system to present information to the user (such as the program guide) and allows the user to interact (select channels) with the STB.

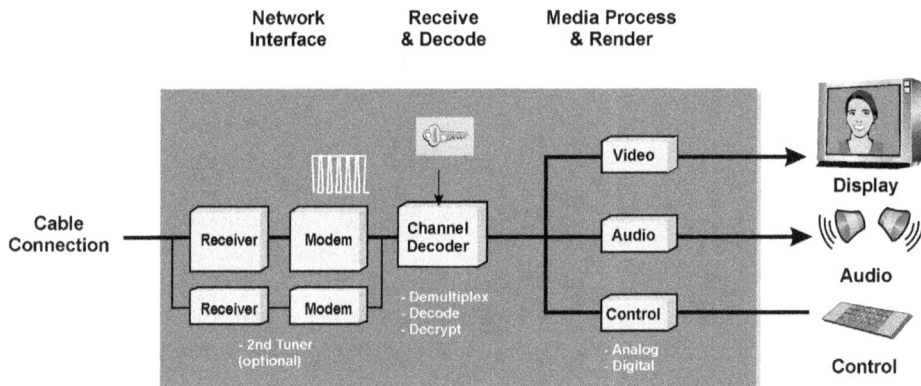

Figure 1.45, TV User Device Functions

Cable access device capabilities include RF tuners, display capability, media processing (video, audio and graphics), security, software applications, accessories, middleware compatibility, media distribution and upgradeability.

Radio Frequency Tuner (RF Tuner)

An RF tuner the parts of an access receiver that converts RF signals to a video and audio output signals. Set top boxes may have one or more tuners. Set top boxes with multi-channel tuners are capable of simultaneously receiving two or more communication channels.

Frequency Selector

The RF tuner selects one of the RF frequency channels from the many incoming RF channels. Cable TV systems can have up to 125 RF channels. Each RF channel can have multiple digital channels (typically 6-10).

Demodulator

A demodulator recovers (extracts) an information signal from a carrier (transport) signal. The output from a demodulator is usually the original baseband information signal format.

Channel Decoder

A channel decoder is a device that convents an incoming channel into its component parts. A channel decoder may separate media channels from control channels.

A channel decoder may include a logical channel selector that can identify, select, and redirect portions of signals from a digital channel. A single digital television channel includes digital video, audio, and control channels.

Multiple RF Tuners

User devices (such as STBs) may only have the capability to receive one type of RF channel at a time (single tuner), or they may be able to receive multiple channels at the same time (multiple tuners). For cable receivers that only have one tuner, the user may be interrupted when data (e.g. program guides) is gathered. For cable receivers that have multiple tuners, the control information can be received and sent without interrupting the viewer's program display.

Display Capability

Display capability is the ability of a device to render images into a display area in different formats. Display capabilities for television viewing devices include size and resolution (SD or HD), the type of video frame formats (interlaced or progressive) and display positioning (scaling and displaying multiple sources).

Display Resolution

Display resolution is the number of pixels (graphic elements) per unit of area. A display with a finer grid contains more pixels, and therefore has a higher resolution, capable of reproducing more detail in an image. The most common resolution formats include standard definition (SD), high-definition (HD) 1k-2k, and Ultra-High Resolution (UHD) 4k. The actual resolution for each of these formats (SD, HD, UHD) can vary slightly by region and type of device.

The consumers access to display resolution has become a bit blurry. Some key factors include content resolution (source), broadcasted resolution (transmission), access device resolution (receive and reformat), display device resolution (display). The optimal situation is where the source content, broadcast transmission, receiving device, and display device all have the same resolution.

Unfortunately, the original content may be low resolution format, broadcast transmission systems may not have HD or UHD capability, and access devices (e.g. set top boxes) may not be upgraded to higher resolution formats. To solve this challenge, TVs or their access devices may automatically convert (upscale) the resolution to the higher format (filling in additional display pixels) resulting in a crisp picture with some distortions.

Figure 1.46 shows some TV display resolution formats. Standard definition (SD) TVs have resolutions of 640 x 480 (NTSC) or 720 x 576 (PAL) resolution with a 4:3 aspect ratio. High Definition (HD) TVs have 1280 x 720 or 1920 x 1080 resolution with a 16:9 aspect ratio (wide). Ultra High Definition 4K (UHD 4K) has 3840 x 2160 resolution with a 16:9 aspect ratio and Ultra High Definition 8K (UHD 8K) has 7680 x 4320 resolution with 16:9 aspect ratio.

Resolution Format	Resolution	Aspect Ratio
Standard Definition (SD)	640 x 480 (NTSC), 720 x 576 (PAL)	4:3 aspect ratio
High Definition (HD)	1280 x 720, 1920 x 1080	16:9 aspect ratio
Ultra High Definition (UHD 4K)	3840 x 2160	16:9 aspect ratio
Ultra High Definition (UHD 8K)	7680 x 4320	16:9 aspect ratio

Figure 1.46, Display Resolution Formats

Aspect Ratios

Aspect ratio is the ratio of a number of items (such as pixels on a screen) compared to the width and height of those items. The aspect ratio determines the frame shape of an image. The aspect ratio of the NTSC (analog television) standard is 4:3 for conventional monitors such as home television sets, and 16:9 for HDTV.

Frame Formats - Interlacing and Progressive

Frame formats are the types and sequence of images that are used to create a moving picture. Frame formats can be field interlacing (portions of the images appear in successive frames) or progressive (each image contains all the image content).

Field interlacing is the process used to create a single video frame by overlapping two pictures where one picture provides the odd lines and the other picture provides the even lines. Field interlacing was used to reduce the amount of transmission bandwidth needed to send a video signal. Odd and even line field interlacing was created to reduce flicker. Progressive frame formats send a complete image for each frame.

Refresh Rates

Refresh rate is the number of frames per second that a display can be redrawn (updated). Faster screen updating may reduce motion blur.

Blur in televisions display may be caused by the amount of time it takes for pixels to change color (response time.) Some types of displays (such as LCD and LED) have slower pixel response times.

Upscaling

Upscaling is the process of converting media to a higher resolution format (such as from HD to UHD). The upscaling process can vary from low processing solutions (duplicating image bits in adjacent pixels) to image analysis and enhancement. For example, upscaling software can analyze an image to determine types of objects (such as a person.) Once the type of object is known (such as skin), the process of adding additional pixels can be chosen based on key characteristics (skin tones.)

Video Outputs

TV access devices may contain multiple video outputs including composite, s-video, RF channel, SCART, and HDMI digital.

Composite video is a single electrical signal that contains luminance, color, and synchronization information. NTSC, PAL, and SECAM all are examples of composite video formats.

Separate video (S-video) is a set of video signals that represent luminance and color information. The separation of intensity and color information provides for a higher quality video signal than composite video.

Syndicat des Constructeurs d'Appareils Radiorécepteurs et Téléviseurs (SCART) is a 21 pin connector that includes multiple types of video signal formats including component video allowing for higher quality analog video signal connections.

An RF output is the selected channel (received channel) that is modulated on to a TV channel (typically channel 3 or 4). Remodulation of the received signal in the set top box for the TV set to demodulate it again can add some distortion.

High Definition Multimedia Interface (HDMI) is a high-speed digital data connection type that combines a high quality digital video interface (DVI) connection along with the security protocol HDCP. HDMI has the ability to determine if security processes are available on the DVI connection and, if not, the HDMI interface can reduce the quality (lower resolution) of the digital video signal.

Security

Security for CATV access devices (such as set top boxes) is ensures content that is accessed by the STB is not copied or used in an unauthorized way by the user. Set top boxes commonly include conditional access control, smart cards, and content protection software to ensure the content is used in its authorized form.

Conditional Access Client

A conditional access client is software program that identifies authorized services and enables a viewing device to receive them. The conditional access client software may be provided by a 3rd party security company which is installed on the customers access device (set top box.)

Cablecard or Smart Card

A Cablecard or smart card is a portable credit card size device that can store and process information that is unique to the owner or manager of the smart card. When the card is inserted into a smart card socket, it transfers information between the electronic device and the card. Smart cards can be used to identify and validate the user of a service. They can also be used as storage devices to hold media, such as messages and pictures.

Smart card software can also be embedded (included) in the set top box to form a virtual smart card. A virtual smart card is a software program and associated secret information on a users device (such as a TV set top box) that can store and process information from another device (a host) to provide access control and decrypt/encrypt information that is sent to and/or from the device.

Digital Rights Management (DRM)

A digital rights management client is a computer, hardware device or software program that is configured to request digital rights management (DRM) services from a network. An example of a DRM client is a software program (module) that is installed (loaded) into a converter box (e.g. set top box) that can request and validate information between the system and the device in which the software is installed.

DRM may be implemented by software and/or hardware. Secure micro-processors contain cryptographic algorithms, such as DES, AES or PKI. The secure microprocessor that is used for decryption may be a separate device or it can be a processing module that is located within another computing device (such as a DSP).

Media Processing

Media processing is the operations used to transfer, store or manipulate media (voice, data or video). The processing of media ranges from the play-back of voice messages to modifying video images to wrap around graphic objects (video warping). Media processing in set top boxes includes video processing, audio processing and graphics processing.

Video Processing

Video processing is the methods that are used to convert and/or modify video signals from one format into another form using signal processing. An example of video processing is the decoding of MPEG video and the conversion of the video into a format that can be displayed on a television monitor (e.g. PAL or NTSC video or a DVI digital stream on an HDMI connection).

Audio Processing

Audio processing is the methods that are used to convert and/or modify audio signals from one format into another form using signal processing. An example of audio processing is the decoding of compressed audio (MP3 or AAC) and converting it into multiple channels of surround sound audio (5.1 audio).

Graphics Processing

Graphics processing is the methods that are used to convert and/or modify image objects from one format into another form. An example of graphics processing the conversion of text (e.g. subtitles) into bitmapped images that can be presented onto a television display (on screen display).

Device Software

The access device software includes an operating system, embedded software, and downloadable applications.

Operating System (OS)

An access device operating system is a group of software programs and routines that directs the operation of a microprocessor (a computing chip) and assists programs in performing their functions. The operating system software is responsible for coordinating and allocating system resources. This includes transferring data to and from memory, processor, and peripheral devices. Software applications use the operating system to gain access to these resources as required.

Embedded Applications

Embedded applications are programs that are stored (encapsulated) within a device. An example of an embedded application is a navigation browser (program guide) that is included as part of a television set top box.

Downloadable Applications (TV Apps)

Downloaded applications are software programs that are requested and transferred from the system when needed. A loader application (the loader is an embedded application) is used to request and transfer applications from the system. Native applications are software instructions that are written in the language used by the device operating system. Native applications need to be customized for each version of the device software. Virtual applications are software instructions that are written in another language to perform applications using an interpreter program (e.g. Javascript). Virtual applications can be created 1x and work on most devices.

Accessories

Cable television accessories are devices or software programs that are used with cable systems or services. Examples of cable television accessories include remote controls, gaming controllers and other human interface devices that are specifically designed to be used with cable television systems and services. These accessories may have dedicated connection points (such as game controllers) or they may share a standard universal serial bus (USB) connection.

Human Interfaces

Human interfaces define how devices such as remote controls, keyboards, game pads, video cameras, and other devices communicate with the access devices. Human interfaces may use infrared or radio communications. Consumer infrared (CIR) remote control devices may use industry standard protocols RC-5 or RC-6 (new advanced features). TV remotes may be replaced by soft TV remote apps on smartphones.

Cable Ready Televisions

Cable ready television is a video display device (a television) that is capable of receiving and displaying channels from a cable television system without the need for external adapters or devices. Cable ready televisions can be analog or digital cable ready.

Cable RF Channels

To be analog cable ready, the tuner or receiver needs to be capable of adjusting its frequency and demodulating cable RF television channels. Beyond ***

Demodulator

A demodulator is a circuit or a device that recovers (extracts) an information signal from a carrier (transport) signal. The output from a demodulator is usually the original baseband information signal format.

CableCard Slot

To be digital cable ready, the television has a Cablecard slot so the television can decode encrypted channels. Digital cable ready televisions may have RF connections or Ethernet only (e.g. for hotels).

Smart Televisions (Smart TVs)

A smart TV (also called a connected TV) includes access to online service through an Internet connection. Online services can be accessed through software programs (apps) that may be pre-installed and/or downloaded. The installation and distribution of apps can generate promotion, activation, and service revenue sharing opportunities for the TV manufacturer and the App and service providers.

Smart TV manufacturers may create platforms that allow for the creation and distribution of apps that are proprietary to their televisions.

Hospitality Televisions

Hospitality televisions contain additional features and connections including content protection system and data connection controls. Hospitality TVs are used in private television networks such as hotels, hospitals, and cruise ships.

Because these TVs may have access to premium content, they may contain additional an content protection such as Pro:Idiom. Pro:Idiom is an end to end content protection system that is included on a media channel which requires decoding by the television or viewing device. Pro:Idiom is setup to extend content protection from the private TV system headend content source to the TVs that have access to the premium content.

Hospitality TVs have the capability of redirecting the remote control capability to another device such as a STB through a serial peripheral interface (SPI) data line (RJ12). This enables the system operator to limit features and provide additional access controls such as redirecting the initial display to a welcome channel or providing interactive access to billing services.

Set-Top box (Cable Converters)

Cable converters, commonly called "set-top boxes" (STB) are electronic devices that convert an incoming cable television signals into a form that can be displayed on a video device, typically a television or computer. The STB is typically located in a customer's home to enable the reception of and/or interaction with services on the customer's television or computer. In digital cable systems, a set-top box is also used to convert digital video (e.g., MPEG2) into standard NTSC, PAL, or HDMI video formats that are used for televisions.

STB contain an RF tuner/receiver that adapts the physical transmission formats from cable networks (analog or digital RF channels) into a format that can be processed by the cable STB. This The STB may contain multiple tuners to allow the STB to receive television programming while it is receiving information from other channels (such as the television programming guide).

A microprocessor controls the overall operation of the STB. It communicates with various types of memory that range from short term random access memory that enables the uP to process instructions to unchangeable read only memory that holds the operating system instructions.

The uP also monitors and manages interface controls such as channel display, TV remotes, keyboards, and accessory connectors.

Security in STBs may include embedded security (chips or downloadable content protection systems) or external security devices (Cablecards or Smart Cards).

The STB uses purpose digital signal processors (DSPs) to convert and manipulate the media such as MPEG streams into their digital video and audio components.

The audio visual (AV) interface provides video and audio signals in formats that can be used by user devices (TVs, DVRs). This may include composite video (RGB), RF connectors (modulate on channel 3 or 4), or HDMI digital connection.

Figure 1.47 shows a basic hardware architecture diagram for a cable set top box (STB). This diagram shows that a cable STB is composed of tuner/receiver components, a microprocessor (uP), memory components, media processors, audio/visual interfaces and user interface controls. The tuner/receiver components adapt the physical transmission formats from cable networks (analog or digital RF channels) into a format that can be processed by the cable STB. The microprocessor controls the overall operation of the STB. The media processor is a special purpose digital signal processor that can convert and manipulate the media (such as converting MPEG). Cable STBs have multiple types of memory that range from short term random access memory that enables the uP to process instructions to unchangeable read only memory that holds the operating system instructions. The audio/visual interfaces adapt the media into formats that can be displayed or heard by the user. The user interface contains displays, keypads and remote control interfaces to allow the user to interact with the STB.

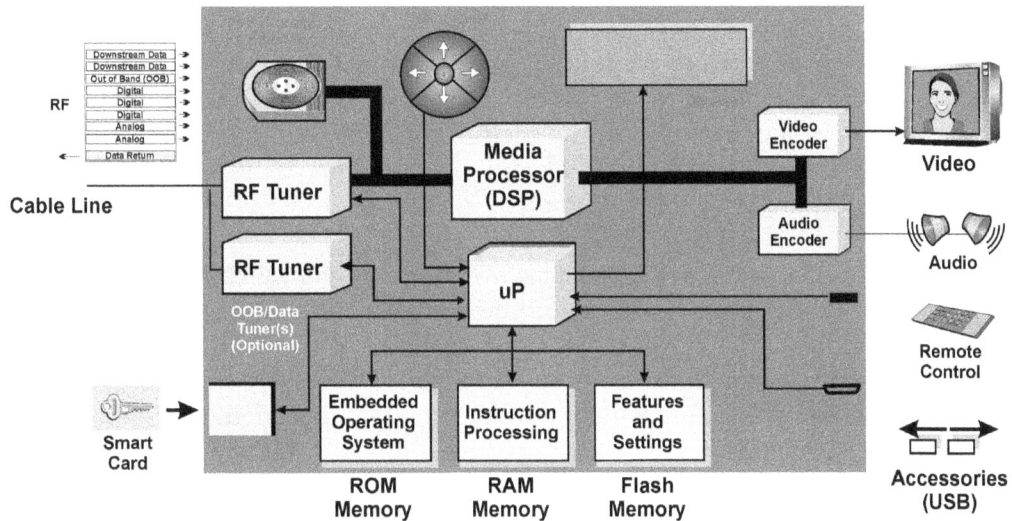

Figure 1.47, Cable Set top Box Hardware

Some cable set top boxes have the capability of receiving and processing signals from other broadcast systems. These hybrid set top boxes (HSTB) are electronic devices that adapt multiple types of communications mediums (RF or data signals) to formats that are accessible by the end user. The use of HSTBs allows a viewer to get direct access to broadcast content from other systems, such as satellite systems, digital terrestrial television (DTT) and/or interactive IPTV via a broadband network.

Cable Modems

A cable modem converts RF signals from the cable system into a standard data format that can be used by computers and converts data signals from a computer into a form that can be routed back to the data network. Cable modems select and decode high data-rate signals on the cable television system (CATV) into digital signals that are designated for a specific user.

The cable modem receiver contains a demodulator that converts the low frequency received signal into its original baseband digital form and performs error detection and correction. The modulator converts the digital information from the computer into a format suitable for transfer back to the Internet.

Initially, cable modems were hybrid systems getting data from the cable system and using a telephone line audio modem sending data back.

A control section coordinates the upstream and downstream access operations (called media access control - MAC) of the cable modem. The control section also coordinates the overall operation of the cable modem, including how it interfaces to communication devices. For example, the data may be converted to Ethernet format for communication with a personal computer.

Cable modems contain one or more tuners, a demodulator, a modulator, media access control (MAC) section, and a control section. The tuner converts a selected RF channel (high frequency) to the modem baseband (low frequency) signal. The tuner makes adjustments to frequency (usually between 42 and 850 MHz) for downstream traffic and may convert the upstream traffic to a different RF channel (usually between 5 and 42 MHz).

Cable television systems commonly use some of the upper RF channels for downstream data channel and lower frequency RF channels are used for upstream. The downstream channels can use very efficient QAM modulation, which offers data rates of 30 Mbps to 40 Mbps for each RF channel, and a more robust QPSK modulation is used on the upstream for data rates of approximately 2 Mbps to 4 Mbps.

Newer cable modems can combine and process multiple RF channels (channel bonding) to provide much higher data rates (up to 10 Gbps).

Figure 1.48 shows a block diagram of a cable modem. This diagram shows that a cable modem uses a tuner to convert an incoming 6 MHz or 8 MHz RF channel to a low frequency baseband signal. This signal is demodulated to a digital format, demultiplexed (separated) from other digital channels, and is decompressed to a single data signal. This data signal is connected to a computer typically in Ethernet data format (e.g. 10 Base T Ethernet). Data that is sent to the modem is converted to either audio signals for transfer via a telephone line (hybrid system) or converted to an RF signal for transmission back through the cable network.

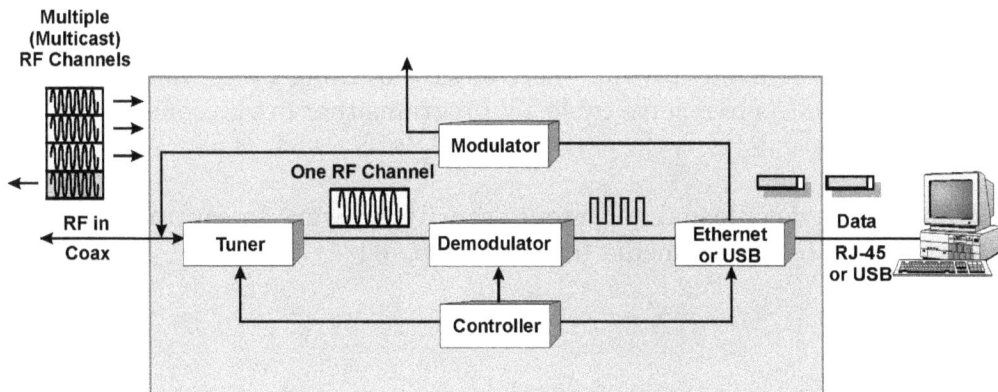

Figure 1.48, Cable Modem

Cable Telephone Adapters

Cable telephone adapters are devices that convert telephone signals into another format (such as digital Internet protocol) that can be transferred on a cable television system. These adapter boxes may provide a single function, such as providing digital telephone service, or they may convert digital signals into several different forms, such as audio, data, and video. When adapter boxes convert into multiple information forms, they may be called multimedia terminal adapters (MTAs) or integrated access devices (IADs).

Digital Media Adapters (DMA)

A digital media adapter (also called a streaming box) is a device or assembly that converts digital media that is in one format (such as Internet Streaming) into another format (such as HDMI digital video). Digital media adapters typically get their media from a wired (WLAN) and/or wireless (WiFi) data connection. While DMAs do not typically include an RF receiver, cable companies may provide these devices or cable TV service apps that run on other DMAs to receive cable TV programs that are streamed (e.g. TV Everywhere).

DMAs contain downloadable content security software to control access to programs and to protect media from being copied.

TV Middleware

TV middleware coordinates the distribution of information between the TV broadcast system (the headend) and end users. This includes system information, access control, system management, application management, protocols, and defined how end user device applications can communicate with other.

System Information

TV middleware coordinates the transmission channel assignments (e.g. which are used for TV, data, and control coordination) and defines the formats on the channels.

Configuration Management

Middleware identifies, monitors, and sets the communication parameters for devices that are connected (attached) to the system.

Program Guides

Middleware manages the continual transfer (broadcasting) of program schedule information for electronic program guides.

Application Program Interfaces (APIs)

Access to other systems and service data is provided by application program interfaces (APIs) for services such as billing system and services.

Security

Middleware allows access to authorized services (conditional access), authentication (verification), and encryption (content protection) systems which can be independent of the middleware software.

Application Management

Middleware performs monitoring, downloading, and managing applications (such as video on demand players, test monitoring clients) and their resources.

Figure 1.49 shows how middleware is used on a cable television system to link the together the media broadcast and management systems (headend) with the end user's equipment (TVs and set top boxes). The middleware software is installed on the headend servers and in the viewing devices (e.g. set top boxes). Middleware functions and capabilities can include protocols, system information, access control, system control, and application management. Middleware protocols may control the transmission, session, and application transfers. Middleware may regularly provide (broadcast) system information that can include channel lists, service lists, and system status information. Middleware may coordinate access control through user identification, authentication, and content encryption. System management may include equipment configuration, monitoring, and diagnostics. Application management may include download control, resource allocation, and application program interfaces (APIs).

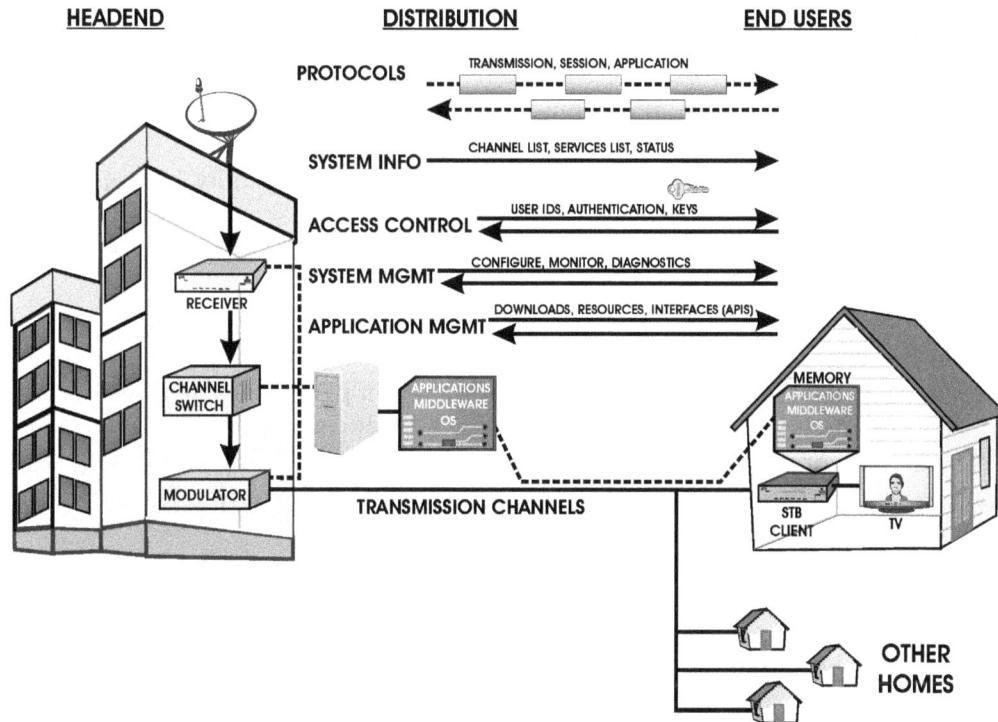

Figure 1.49, CATV Middleware

Access Control and Service Interfaces

Access control involves the identification of users, how to determine which services are authorized for specific users, ways to validate the identify (authentication) of users, when and how media will be protected (encrypted), and coordination of how keys and certificates are distributed.

Middleware systems may identify which methods are available for access control, service authorization, authentication, and encryption. The actual providing of the control is commonly provided by separate conditional access system (CAS) and digital rights management (DRM) systems.

Electronic Program Guide (EPGs)

Electronic program guides (EPGs) provide viewers with an understanding of what content is available to them. Broadcasters face key tradeoffs when designing EPGs which include the amount of descriptive data, display formats, navigation options, and promotional messaging.

Program listings may be display chronologically or they may be organized and filtered based on categories or other criteria. Broadcasters may include graphics and messages with the EPG for promotional purposes such as upcoming movie trailers or ads.

An EPG system starts with gathering program scheduling and descriptive information (metadata). The broadcaster's system processes the information (program scheduling information) and repeatedly transmits the EPG data over one or more broadcast channels. The viewers receiving device (e.g. set top box) captures, decodes, and processes the EPG information for the viewer's display.

Figure 1.50 shows an end-to-end electronic program guide - EPG system. The process starts with the creation of program descriptive information (EPG metadata). The metadata information is gathered from one or more companies by the broadcaster. The metadata is updated with schedule information and transferred to viewers over one or more broadcast channels. The receiving devices (e.g. set top box) in this example gathers and processes the EPG data and displays the guide to the viewer.

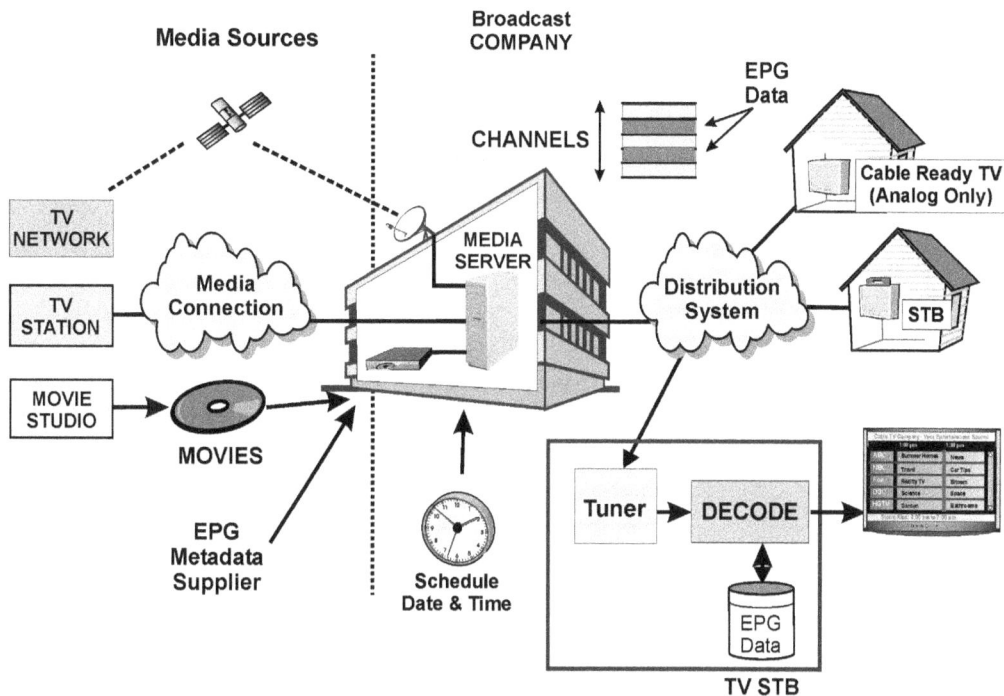

Figure 1.50, Electronic Program Guide System

EPG Data

EPG data can range from basic title, date, and time to detailed descriptions and selectable navigation messages and images. EPG data can include title, schedule information, short descriptions, long descriptions, and other attributes. The amount of EPG data that is included for each program ranges from a few hundred bytes (title only) to tens of kilobytes (long descriptions).

Program title information is typically up to 40 characters long. Schedule information contains date, time, broadcaster identification, and channel information. Short descriptions are typically up to 144 characters and long descriptions can include program summary, show highlights, key actor names, and other descriptive data.

EPG data may also include other program attributes. These can include genre categories, ratings (parental, quality score), and other machine readable information such as media formats (SD, HD). EPG data may also include service access rights which controls who is allowed to view the EPG data and use its services.

EPG Metadata Suppliers

EPG descriptive information (metadata) can come from the content owners, aggregators, independent companies, or other viewers. Some content owners (e.g. movie producers) commonly provide a program media package which include multiple descriptions and additional information.

Program metadata aggregators provide high quality program descriptions on a license fee basis. Alternative suppliers can range from independent companies that write new descriptions to social media sources that create free open program guide information. Program metadata suppliers include Tribune Media, Gemstar-TV (Rovi), and FYI Television.

EPG metadata suppliers may provide descriptive information on a file transfer basis or they may allow for real time access via defined application program interface - API connections.

EPG Data Transmission

EPG data may be transmitted trough one or multiple broadcast transmission channels. In older systems it was sent with other data during the video blanking rescan time. Newer systems send the EPG data in MPEG data streams. Some devices can request EPG data either through the TV broadcast system (return channel) or through the Internet.

EPG data is continuously repeated to allow receivers (e.g. set top boxes) to decode the data when they are on and tuned to broadcast channels. The most recent EPG data is repeated more often.

EPG data may be divided into two or more streams. One stream may be used to provide near program information (current day and next day) and the other stream may be used to transfer far (long term) information. The near stream is repeated more often. The complete transfer of all EPG information should take less than one TV program (about 20 minutes).

Figure 1.51 shows that EPG data may be transmitted through one or multiple broadcast channels and some receiving devices may request the transfer of the EPG data by the broadcaster's return channel or through the Internet.

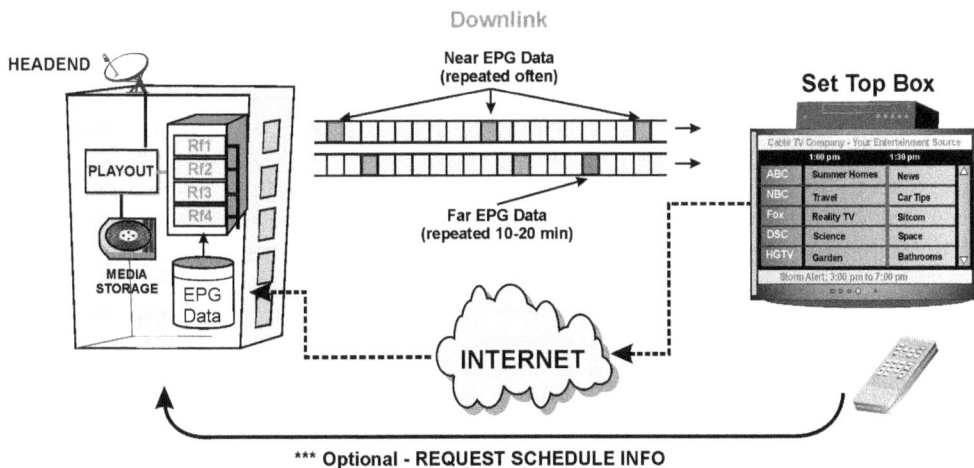

Figure 1.51, EPG Data Transmission

Interactive Program Guides (IPGs)

Interactive program guides (IPGs) allow viewers to choose (navigate to) specific programs in the EPG display. IPGs can vary from simple program selections to interactive filters that dynamically allow the user to filter through program guides by theme, time period, or other criteria.

Recommendation Engines

A recommendation engine is an application that searches through data files or related listings of information (such as television programs) to find matches to categories or items that the person who is searching or viewing programs is likely to be interested in obtaining or viewing.

Application Management

Middleware systems coordinate the installation, operation, and resource allocation for software and communication applications. It defines how applications (programs) to communicate with other applications and services using application protocol interfaces (APIs).

Application program interfaces are defined and documented entry points into a software application where other programs may interact with the application in order to provide customized extensions or perform special processing functions. Typically an API is a public function call that, then itself, calls on the services of the application. In this way, the API hides the underlying details and complexities of the application software making it easier for programmers to add custom functionality.

TV Industry Standards

There are many types of TV industry standards used in cable television systems. Some of the key standards include analog video (NTSC, PAL, SECAM), Digital Video (MPEG) Cable Modem (DOCSIS), Home Media Network (DLNA), Cable Telephony (PacketCable), TV Middleware (OpenCable, MHP), and Hybrid Broadcast Broadband TV (HBBTV).

National Television Standards Committee (NTSC)

The NTSC system is an analog video system that was developed in the United States and is used in many parts of the world. The NTSC system uses analog modulation in which a sync burst precedes the lines of video information. The NTSC system uses 525 lines of resolution (42 are blanking lines) and has a pixel resolution of approximately 148k to 150k pixels.

The NTSC system uses 6 MHz wide radio channels that range from 54 MHz to 88 MHz (for VHF channels 1-6), 174 MHz to 216 MHz (for VHF channels 7-13) and 470 MHz to 806 MHz (for UHF channels 14-69). Initially, the frequency range of 806 MHz to 890 MHz was available for UHF channels 70 to 83. The FCC reallocated these channels for cellular and specialized mobile radio (SMR) use in 1983.

Figure 1.52 demonstrates the operation of the basic NTSC analog television system. The video source is broken into 30 frames per second and converted into multiple lines per frame. Each video line transmission begins with a burst pulse (called a sync pulse) that is followed by a signal that represents color and intensity. The time relative to the starting sync is the position on the line from left to right. Each line is sent until a frame is complete and the next frame can begin. The television receiver decodes the video signal to position and control the intensity of an electronic beam that scans the phosphorus tube ("picture tube") to recreate the display.

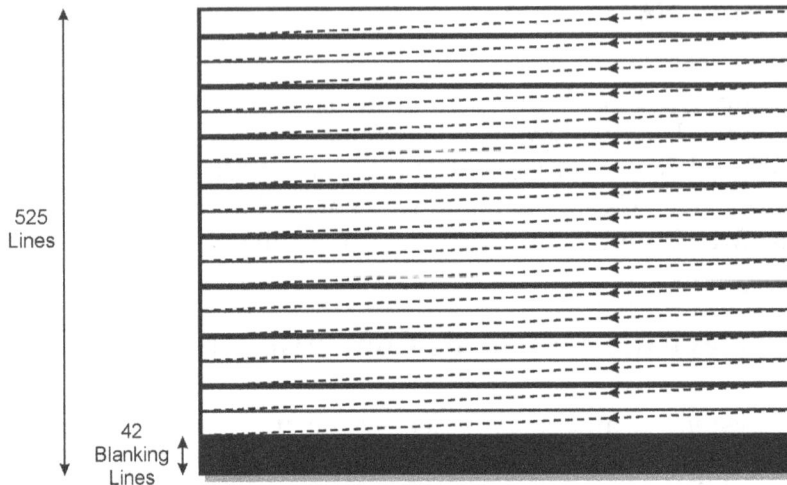

Figure 1.52, NTSC (Analog) Video

Phase Alternating Line (PAL)

The PAL system was developed in the 1980's to provide a common television standard in Europe. PAL is now used in the Middle East and parts of Asia and Africa. The PAL system uses a phase alternation process to enhance the video signal's resistance to chromatic distortions as compared with the NTSC video signal. Although PAL and NTSC systems are similar in function, they are not compatible.

The system provides 625 lines per frame and 50 frames per second. A modified version of PAL (PAL-M) is used for the Brazilian television system. PAL-M provides 525 lines per frame and 60 frames per second. The PAL system uses 7 or 8 MHz wide radio channels.

Figure 1.53 demonstrates the operation of the basic PAL analog television system. The video source is broken into 50 frames per second and converted into 625 lines per frame. Each video line transmission begins with a burst pulse (called a sync pulse) that is followed by a signal that represents color and intensity. The time relative to the starting sync is the position on the line from left to right. Each line is sent until a frame is complete and the next frame can begin. The television receiver decodes the video signal to position and control the intensity of an electronic beam that scans the phosphorus tube ("picture tube") to recreate the display.

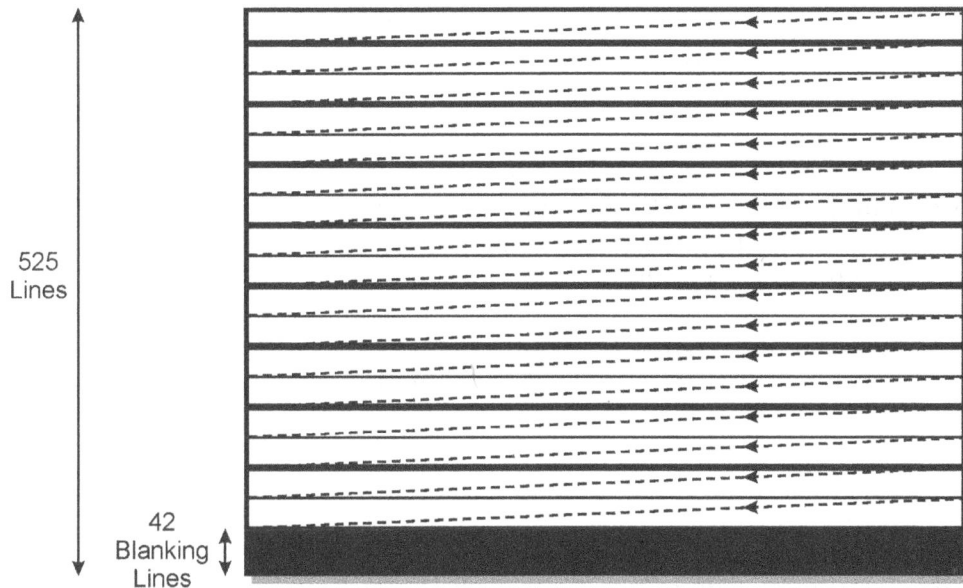

Figure 1.53, PAL (Analog) Video

Sequential Couleur Avec MeMoir (SECAM)

SECAM is an analog color TV system that provides 625 lines per frame and 50 fields per second. This system is similar to PAL and is used in France, the former USSR, the former Eastern Block countries, and some Middle East countries. In order to transmit color the information is transmitted sequentially on alternate lines as a FM signal.

Moving Picture Experts Group (MPEG)

Moving picture experts group (MPEG) standards are digital video encoding processes that coordinates the transmission of multiple forms of media (multimedia). Moving picture experts group (MPEG) is a working committee that defines and develops industry standards for digital video systems. These standards specify the data compression and decompression processes and how they are delivered on digital broadcast systems. MPEG is part of International Standards Organization (ISO). To get MPEG specifications, visit the Motion Pictures Expert Group at http://mpeg.chiariglione.org/

There are various levels of MPEG compression; MPEG-1, MPEG-2, and MPEG-4 (MPEG-3 was merged into MPEG-2.) MPEG-1 compresses by approximately 50 to 1, MPEG-2 compresses up to 100 to 1, and MPEG-4 compresses up to about 200:1. Video compression efficiency and quality continues to improve with multiple MPEG-4 compression types.

The MPEG standards define a transmission stream (MPEG-TS) format that allows multiple MPEG streams to share a single transmission line.

MPEG-1

MPEG-1 is the original multimedia transmission system that allowed combining and synchronizing of multiple media types (e.g. digital audio and digital video). MPEG-1 was primarily developed for CDROM multimedia applications.

MPEG-2

MPEG-2 is a frame oriented multimedia transmission system that allows for compression, combining, and synchronizing of multiple media types onto broadcast channels. MPEG-2 video compression can provide SD video quality with a data rate of approximately 3.8 Mbps.

MPEG-4

MPEG-4 is a digital multimedia compression and transmission standard that was designed to allow for packet based interactive digital television services of object based media. It allows for multiple video compression types allowing it to have more than 200:1 compression ratio. It also allows for the transmission of separate media objects (such as text, images, and video) which provides for better text display (no fuzzy edges) and motion graphics capabilities (animation).

The original video compression format was part 2 of the MPEG-4 specification which offered approximately the same compression ratio as MPEG-2 system (about 100:1). To increase efficiency, MPEG-4 part 10 advanced video coding (AVC) was created in 2010 which approximately doubled the compression radio (200:1).

The high efficiency video coding (HEVC) specification (H.265) released in 2015 provides an increase in the compression efficiency as compared to MPEG-4 part 10 AVC. The increased compression efficiency comes from analyzing larger graphic areas within frame images.

MPEG Dynamic Streaming over HTTP (MPEG-DASH)

MPEG dynamic adaptive streaming over HTTP (DASH) is a process that uses existing Internet protocol to coordinate how digital videos can be transferred through the Internet when data transmission rates vary (variable bandwidth). It his similar to HTTP live streaming (HLS) which works by dividing the stream into small HTTP data segments which can be sent at different data rates. This allows a MPEG-DASH receiver (client) can continually adapt to changing bandwidth conditions.

MPEG Transport Stream (MPEG-TS)

MPEG transport streams are the combining (multiplexing) of multiple program channels (typically digital video channels) onto a signal communication channel. Cable television systems commonly use an MPEG transport stream (MPEG-TS) to transfer multiple programs on each RF transmission channel. MPEG transport streams (MPEG-TS) use a fixed length packet size and a packet identifier identifies each transport packet within the transport stream. A packet identifier in an MPEG system identifies the packetized elementary streams (PES) of a program channel. A program (such as a television show) is usually composed of multiple PES channels (e.g. video and audio).

Figure 1.54 shows how MPEG systems have evolved over time. This diagram shows that the original MPEG specification (MPEG-1) developed in 1991 offered medium quality digital video and audio at up to 1.2 Mbps, primarily sent via CD ROMs. This standard evolved in 1995 to become MPEG-2, which was used for satellite and cable digital television, along with DVD distribution. The MPEG specification then evolved into MPEG-4 in 1999 to permit multimedia distribution through the Internet. This example shows that work continues with MPEG-7 for object based multimedia and MPEG-21 for digital rights management.

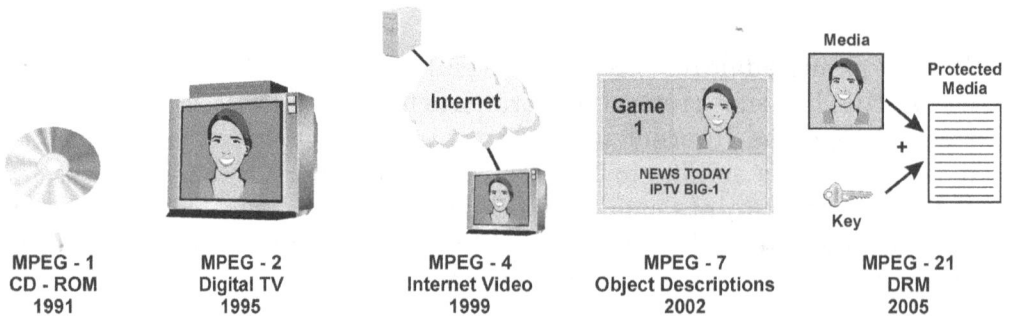

Figure 1.54, Evolution of MPEG

Data Over Cable Service Interface Specifications (DOCSIS)

The data over cable service interface specifications (DOCSIS) is a standard used by cable systems for providing data services (such as broadband Internet) to users. The DOCSIS standard was primarily developed by equipment manufacturers and CATV operators. It details most aspects of data over cable networks including physical layer (modulation types and data rates), medium access control (MAC), data services, and security. The DOCSIS cable modem specifications are available from CableLabs® at www.cablemodem.com/specifications.html

DOCSIS 1.0

DOCSIS 1.0 Version 1.0 is the first industry standard used by cable television systems for providing Internet data services to users. Released in March 1997, the DOCSIS 1.0 Specification defines downstream digital channels that occupy one RF channel (6 MHz) and upstream channels that can range from 200 kHz to 3.2 MHz wide which use a slotted (TDMA) shared access system.

DOCSIS 1.1

DOCSIS 1.1 is a cable television Internet data communication standard related in April 1999 that adds quality of service (QoS) capabilities to DOCSIS 1.0.

DOCSIS 2.0

DOCSIS 2.0 is a cable television Internet data communication specification released December 2001 that adds enhanced upstream communication services to previous DOCSIS versions. It enables synchronous services through added asynchronous code division multiple access (S-CDMA) upstream channel format and provides faster upstream data channels by using RF channel bandwidths of 6.4 MHz.

DOCSIS 3.0

DOCSIS 3.0 is a cable television Internet data communication specification released August 2006 that that includes channel bonding capability to increase maximum data rates and adds IPv6 capability (more Internet addresses.)

DOCSIS 3.1

DOCSIS 3.1 is a cable television Internet data system specification released October 2013 that that increases data transmission rate up to 10 Gbps downstream and 1 Gbps upstream using. It uses more efficient 4096 QAM modulation and adds 20 kHz to 50 kHz orthogonal frequency division multiplexing (OFDM) transmission channels which provides more reliable data transfer rates when there are interfering signals. The RF channel widths are flexible with up to 200 MHz wide.

Full Duplex DOCSIS 3.1

Full duplex DOCSIS 3.1 is a flexible high speed data communication specification developed by Cablelabs in 2016 that provides up to 10 Gbps data transmission in both directions (upstream or downstream.) Full Duplex DOCSIS uses signal cancelling technology to reduce the interference between upstream and downstream signals on the same frequencies [16].

European DOCSIS (EuroDOCSIS)

The DOCSIS standards have been modified by Excentis (formerly tComLabs) to use TV frequency bandwidths defined by European countries (such as 8 MHz for PAL/DVB-C) as compared to 6 MHz bandwidths used in North America (NTSC/ATSC).

Figure 1.55 shows versions of DOCSIS and their key capabilities. DOCSIS 1.0 was the initial cable TV Internet data system using single cable RF channels converted to TDMA data, limited width uplink data channels. DOCSIS 1.1 added quality of service (QoS) capabilities. DOCSIS 2.0 added faster upstream capabilities using coded spread spectrum transmission (S-CDMA). DOCSIS 3.0 added channel bonding capability to increase maximum data rates and adds IPv6 capability (more Internet addresses.) DOCSIS 3.1 increased data transmission rate up to 10 Gbps downstream and 1 Gbps upstream using more efficient and interference resistant OFDM modulation and flexible width RF channels up to 200 MHz wide. Full Duplex DOCSIS 3.1 added flexible high speed data communication providing up to 10 Gbps data transmission in both directions (upstream or downstream) and added interference signal cancelling technology.

Version	Year	Key Features
DOCSIS 1.0	1997	Initial cable TV Internet data system, single cable RF channels converted to TDMA data, limited width uplink data channels.
DOCSIS 1.1	1999	Added quality of service (QoS) capabilities.
DOCSIS 2.0	2001	Added faster upstream capabilities using coded spread spectrum transmission (S-CDMA)
DOCSIS 3.0	2006	Added channel bonding capability to increase maximum data rates and adds IPv6 capability (more Internet addresses.)
DOCSIS 3.1	2013	Increased data transmission rates up to 10 Gbps downstream and 1 Gbps upstream using more efficient and interference resistant OFDM modulation and flexible width RF channels up to 200 MHz wide
Full Duplex DOCSIS 3.1	2016	Added flexible high speed data communication providing up to 10 Gbps data transmission in both directions (upstream or downstream) and added interference signal cancelling technology.

Figure 1.55, DOCSIS Evolution

Digital Living Network Alliance (DLNA)

Digital living network alliance is an industry standard that allows media devices to discover, connect and communicate with each other over a home network. DLNA certified products should be able to work with each other regardless of manufacturer or the type of home network used (WiFi, wired, HomePlug, or others). More information about DLNA can be found at www.DLNA.org.

DLNA devices are discoverable with each other and are ready to use out of the box. Device and service discovery and control enables devices on the home network to automatically self configure networking properties (such as an IP address), discover the presence and capabilities of other devices on the network, and control and collaborate with these devices in a uniform and consistent manner.

DLNA's protected streaming guidelines allow consumers to securely share commercial content between devices within the home network, but not with third parties. Protected streaming specifies a global standard for protecting content streaming between two devices within the home network, ensuring that commercial content is protected from piracy and illegitimate redistribution.

DLNA divides consumer devices into key types of domains, including computers, mobile and consumer electronics. DLNA defines devices that can process media as home network devices (HNDs). HNDs can be divided into classes, which include media servers, controllers, players, renderers and printers.

Digital Media Server (DMS)

A digital media server is a computing device that can process requests for and deliver digital media. A DMS may perform the acquisition, storage and transfer of media content, such as videos, pictures and audio files. DMS functions may be included in advanced set top boxes, digital video recorders (DVRs) and digital tuners.

Digital Media Controller (DMC)

A digital media controller is a device or software application that discovers and coordinates access to media on digital media servers for further direction to digital media rendering (DMR) devices. Examples of DMCs include televisions, computers and interactive remote controls.

Digital Media Player (DMP)

A digital media player is a device or software application that can request and receive media such as video, audio or images, and convert it into a form that can be experienced by humans. DMP devices include personal computers with media player software, television monitors and multimedia mobile telephones.

Digital Media Renderer (DMR)

A digital media renderer is a device or software application that can display media to a viewer after the media has been processed by, or made available to another device. DMR devices include video monitors, digital displays and audio speakers.

Digital Media Printer (DMPr)

A digital media printer is a device or a software application that can convert media into a form that can be transferred to printed formats. Examples of DMPrs include photograph printers, inkjet printers and laser printers.

Figure 1.56 shows the evolution of the digital living network alliance (DLNA) specifications. The original DLNA 1.0 specification was released in 2004 described the basic system, protocols, media formats, and device types. DLNA 1.5 released in 2006 added new device classes, capabilities, and media format protocols. DLNA 2.0 that released in 2015 added support for electronic program guides (EPGs), content synchronization, along with new security capabilities. DLNA 3.0 was released in 2015 provided for faster response time and support for HEVC digital media. DLNA 2016 released in 2016 improved compatibility for connected TV devices and provided new energy power saving modes.

Version	Year	Key Features
DLNA 1.0	2004	Basic System, Protocols, Media Formats, Device Types
DLNA 1.5	2006	Device Classes, Capabilities, Media Format Protocols
DLNA 2.0	2015	EPG, DVR, Content Sync, Security
DLNA 3.0	2015	Faster Response Time, HEVC Digital Media
DLNA 4.0	2016	Improved Connected TV Interoperability, Energy Power Saving

Figure 1.56, Digital Living Network Alliance (DLNA) Standard Versions

PacketCable(tm)

PacketCable is a suite of interoperability specifications to that enables devices within a packetized telephony-over-cable network to function with each other even if they are provided by many vendors.

PacketCable delivers services using standard IP packet data communication over managed IP network. The PacketCable system can sit on top of the DOCSIS system, allowing cable companies to transform their cable data networks into advanced service PacketCable systems.

IP Multimedia System (IMS)

The PacketCable system is based on an IP multimedia subsystem (IMS) that is an enhancement of session initiation protocol (SIP). The PacketCable system is able to provide voice, data and video services over the IP network, while assigning and managing different levels of quality of service (QoS).

The PacketCable system has evolved from a basic packet data communication system to an advanced high-speed multimedia communication system. The initial PacketCable 1.0 core services allowed for cable telephony (VoIP) services. A PacketCable Multimedia version was released to provide mixed media (multimedia) services. The PacketCable 2.0 version merged voice, data and video services, using modular system architecture.

OpenCable(tm)

OpenCable is a communication system middleware industry standard (between the headend and devices) that is managed by CableLabs and designed to provide advanced television and data communication services. The OpenCable system has a reference design with standard interfaces including headend, core network and consumer product interfaces.

OpenCable defines the protocols (commands and processes) that are used to provide features and services. The OpenCable systems application program interface (API) defines how devices can transfer information to and from the Cable TV system. The OpenCable system also defines the security processes that include how to setup and manage CableCARDs.

The OpenCable industry standard is developed by CableLabs. Testing and certification processes are also provided by CableLabs to help ensure that products designed to the OpenCable specification perform their expected operations. The CableLabs industry specification is primarily created by Cable companies as membership to CableLabs is limited to cable service providers (a closed industry standards process).

CableCARD

The OpenCable system uses a portable credit card size device (CableCARD) that can store and process information that is unique to the owner or manager of the cable card. When the card is inserted into a cable card socket (such as into a set top box), electrical pads on the card connect it to transfer information between the electronic device and the card. Cable cards are used to identify and validate the user or a service and may contain decryption keys that allow for the descrambling of cable transport channels.

Tru2Way System

Tru2Way is a middleware industry specification (part of the OpenCable industry specifications) developed by CableLabs for the television industry which defines how real time interactive services can be provided on a Cable TV system.

Digital Video Broadcasting (DVB)

Digital video broadcasting (DVB) is a standards group that has created specifications for cable, wireless, and satellite broadcast TV systems. DVB-C is the specifications for cable TV systems and DVB-MPH is the specification for its TV middleware. DVB specifications are primarily used in Europe, Asia, and South America and are available from the Digital Video Broadcast standards group at https://www.dvb.org/standards

Digital Video Broadcasting Cable (DVB-C)

The digital video broadcasting cable specification defines RF transmission channels, modulation, and channel coding. DVB-C uses MPEG video (MPEG-2 and MPEG-4), uses multiple levels of QAM modulation, and multiple types of channel coding for error detection and recovery.

DVB-C2 is an enhanced version of the DVB-C broadcast cable specification which includes more efficient modulation and channel coding methods to increase the system capacity by over 30% in typical systems. A DVB-C2 8 MHz RF channel can transfer 83.1 Mbps [17].

Multimedia Home Platform (MHP)

Multimedia home platform is an industry middleware industry standard used in the digital video broadcasting (DVB) system. It defines the communication of the DVB system with the integrated receiver device (IRD) and other set top box receivers that have MHP capability. MHP is designed to allow the user to access additional interactive services such as Internet browsing and electronic programming guides.

Hybrid Broadcast Broadband (HbbTV)

Hybrid broadcast broadband television (HbbTV) is an industry standard that defines how to mix of broadcast media (satellite, cable, local broadcast) transmission with Internet connections to a single viewing device. Hybrid broadcasting allows for the inclusion of media and links in the broadcast signal which can be used to enhance the viewer's TV media experience. When a viewer interacts with the embedded objects (such as links), their TV can be redirected to other sources (such as Interactive ads). For more information, visit the HbbTV association https://www.hbbtv.org.

HbbTV allows broadcasters to add new services and interactive capabilities to their system to better compete with new types of broadcast companies such as OTT and mobile video. HBBTV can be used to enhance programming services (new content) and provide for interactive services (return channels through the Internet). HbbTV services include teletext, video on demand, EPG, interactive advertising, content personalization, and social networking.

HBBTV is primarily a open platform software solution that can be used TV equipment manufacturers, middleware software developers, and TV broadcasters. Software in installed in the head end and in the receiving device (such as set top boxes). HbbTV allows the user to have a seamless entertainment experience.

HbbTV systems have a collection of software components that may include JavaScript™, CSS, and HTML documents. This allows them to merge new content with broadcast media with well understood Internet content and applications. HbbTV delivery options include broadcast, switched channels, and repetitive broadcasts (carousels).

Other standards groups have merged with HbbTV including Open IPTV Forum (2014) and Smart TV Alliance (2016).

HbbTV 1.0

HbbTV 1.0 is the initial hybrid broadcast broadband TV specification which defines how multiple media sources could be received by one device with a single integrated program guide. It described how broadcasted content could be enhanced with personalized content.

HbbTV 1.5

HbbTV 1.5 is an expansion of the HbbTV specification which added dynamic adaptive streaming capability (MPEG-DASH), multiple DRM, and enhanced program guide schedule information (SI EIT).

HbbTV 2.0

HbbTV 2.0 is an evolution of the HbbTV specification that ads support for multiple TV, Smartphone, PC, and tablet devices, provided new interactive applications that includes more program information, voting, play to screen, and others. HbbTV also includes HEVC and Ultra HD streaming capability, support for multiple languages, and advanced advertising capabilities.

Figure 1.57 shows how HbbTV industry standard has evolved. The original HbbTV specification was released in 2006 which defined how multiple media sources could be accessed by an integrated program guide on a single device. HbbTV 1.5 became available in 2012 which allowed for adaptive streaming, multiple DRM systems, and improvements in program guide information. HbbTV 2.0 was published in 2015 which added support for HEVC and Ultra HD, companion device support, multiple languages, and more HTML5 user experience options.

Version	Year	Key Features
HbbTV 1.0	2006	Initial specification, multiple media sources, embedded content & links, and integrated program guide.
HbbTV 1.5	2012	Dynamic adaptive streaming for HTTP (DASH), multiple DRM, and enhanced program guide schedule information (SI EIT).
HbbTV 2.0	2015	Support for HEVC and Ultra HD, companion device support, multiple languages, and more HTML5 user experience options.

Figure 1.57, Hybrid Broadcast and Broadband (HbbTV) Versions

References:

1. "How Cable Television Works," www.HowStuffworks.com, 7 November 2006.
2. Ibid.
3. Ibid.
4. Ibid.
5. Supercomm 2001, "Fujitsu Presentation", 8 June 2001, Atlanta, GA.
6. "How Cable Television Works," www.Howstuffworks.com, 22 November, 2006.
7. FCC Report on Video Competition, 18th Report, 17 January 2017, page 5.
8. "US Digital Ad Spending to Surpass TV this Year," eMarketer, September 13, 2016.
9. CableLabs Blog, Full Duplex DOCSIS, 2017 - www.cablelabs.com/full-duplex-docsis/
10. "How Cable Television Works," www.Howstuffworks.com, 2 August, 2001
11. "The Historical Development of HDTV", Princeton University, https://www.princeton.edu/~ota/disk2/1990/9007/900704.PDF.
12. Wilson, Eric and Shirali, Chet, "Adapting DOCSIS for Broadband Wireless-Access Systems," http://www.csdmag.com/main/2000/10/0010feat3.htm, 10 August, 2001.
13. FCC NPRM, FCC 15-138, https://apps.fcc.gov/edocs_public/attachmatch/FCC-15-138A1.pdf.
14. "ITU G.hn - Broadband Home Networking". In Berger, Lars T.; Schwager, Andreas; Pagani, Pascal; Schneider, Daniel M. MIMO Power Line Communications: Narrow and Broadband Standards, EMC, and Advanced Processing. Devices, Circuits, and Systems. CRC Press. 2014. ISBN 9781466557529.
15. FCC Report on Video Competition, 18th Report, 17 January 2017.
16. http://www.cablelabs.com/full-duplex-docsis-3-1-technology-raising-the-ante-with-symmetric-gigabit-service.
17. DVB Scene Magazine, Sep 2013, https://www.dvb.org/resources/public/scene/DVB-SCENE42.pdf

Appendix 1 - Acronyms

3DTV-3 Dimensional Television
AAC-Advanced Audio Codec
AVOD-Advertising Video on Demand
AIMS-Alliance for IP Media Solutions
APIs-Application Program Interfaces
Apps-Application Programs
ASI-Asynchronous Digital Interface
BS-Base Stations
Gbps-Billion Bits per Second
CMTS-Cable Modem Termination System
CATV-Cable Television
CDMA-Code Division Multiple Access
COTS-Common Off-The-Shelf
CAS-Conditional Access System
CBR-Constant Bit Rate
CAM-Content Asset Management
CDN-Content Distribution Networks
CPRM-Content Protection for Recordable Media
cpm-Cost per Thousand
CNI-Country Network Identifier
CPE-Customer Premises Equipment
DOCSIS-Data Over Cable Service Interface Specifications

DLNA-Digital Living Network Alliance
DMC-Digital Media Controller
DMP-Digital Media Player
DMPr-Digital Media Printer
DMR-Digital Media Renderer
DMS-Digital Media Server
DSP-Digital Signal Processor
DSL-Digital Subscriber Line
DTT-Digital Terrestrial Television
DTCP-Digital Transmission Content Protection
DVB-Digital Video Broadcasting
DVB-C-Digital Video Broadcasting Cable
DVD-Digital Video Disk
DVI-Digital Video Interface
DVR-Digital Video Recorder
DCAS-Downloadable Conditional Access System
ENG.-Electronic News Gathering
EPG-Electronic Program Guide
EAS-Emergency Alert System
ETV-Enhanced Television
EuroDOCSIS-European DOCSIS
XML-Extensible Markup Langague
FCC-Federal Communications Commission
fps-Frames Per Second
GOP-Group of Pictures
HD-High Definition

HDCP-High Definition Content Protection
HDMI-High Definition Multimedia Interface
HDTV-High Definition Television
HEVC-High Efficiency Video Coding
HND-Home Network Device
HbbTV-Hybrid Broadcast Broadband
HFC-Hybrid Fiber Coax
HSTB-Hybrid Set Top Box
IPPV-Impulse Pay Per View
ISM-Industrial, Scientific, and Medical
IADs-Integrated Access Devices
IRD-Integrated Receiver and Decoder
IP-Intellectual Property
IPG-Interactive Program Guide
IPG-Interactive Program Guide
iTV-Interactive Television
ISO-International Standards Organization
IP-Internet Protocol
IPTV-Internet Protocol Television
IP Video-Internet Protocol Video
ISP-Internet Service Provider
IMS-IP Multimedia System
LASER-Light Amplification for the Stimulation of Radiation
LED-Light Emitting Diode
LCD-Liquid Crystal Display
LMDS-Local Multichannel Distribution Service
LPTV-Low Power TV
MAC-Media Access Control
MAM-Media Asset Management

uP-Microprocessor
MoCA-Multimedia over Coax Alliance
MoDem-Modulator/Demodulator
MPEG-Moving Picture Experts Group
MP3-Moving Picture Experts Group Layer 3
MPEG-DASH-MPEG Dynamic Adaptive Streaming over HTTP
MPEG-TS-MPEG Transport Stream
MMDS-Multichannel Multipoint Distribution Service
MVPD-Multichannel Video Programming Distributor
MHP-Multimedia Home Platform
MTa-Multimedia Terminal Adapter
MPTS-Multi-Program Transport Stream
NTSC-National Television Standards Committee
NVOD-Near Video on Demand
OVP-Online Video Providers
OS-Operating System
OLAN-Optical Local Area Networks
ONU-Optical Network Units
OFDM-Orthogonal Frequency Division Multiplexing
OTT-Over the Top Television
PES-Packetized Elementary Streams
POF-Passive Optical Fiber
PPV-Pay Per View
PAL-Phase Alternating Line
PLC-Power Line Carrier
PID-Program Identifier Code
PEG-Public, Education, and

Government
QAM-Quadrature Amplitude Modulation
QPSK-Quadrature Phase Shift Keying
QoS-Quality of Service
RSS-Really Simple Syndication
RGB-Red Green Blue
SECAM-Sequential Couleur Avec MeMoir
SDI-Serial Digital Interface
STB-Set Top Box
SMPTE-Society of Motion Picture and Television Engineers
SD-Standard Definition
SVOD-Subscription Video on Demand
SVS-Switched Video Service
S-CDMa-Synchronous Code Division Multiple Access
TV Apps-Television Applications
tCommerce-Television Commerce
TDMa-Time Division Multiple Access
TVOD.-Transactional Video on Demand
UHD-Ultra High Definition
UHF-Ultra High Frequency
URL-Universal Resource Locator
USB-Universal Serial Bus
UTP-Unshielded Twisted Pair
VBR-Variable Bit Rate
VHF-Very High Frequency
VOD-Video on Demand
VPN-Virtual Private Network
VoIP-Voice Over Internet Protocol
WLAN-Wireless Local Area Networks
WMTS-Wireless Modem Termination System

Index

Digital HDTV, 5, 37, 162
Digital Living Network Alliance (DLNA), 143, 152-154, 169
Digital Media Adapter (DMA), 54, 134, 168
Digital Media Controller (DMC), 153, 169
Digital Media Player (DMP), 153, 169
Digital Media Printer (DMPr), 153, 169
Digital Media Renderer (DMR), 153, 169
Digital Media Server (DMS), 152, 169
Digital Program Insertion (DPI), 80, 165
Digital Rights Management (DRM), 124-125, 137, 148, 158-159
Digital Signal Processor (DSP), 125, 130
Digital Storage Media (DSM), 76
Digital Television (DTV), 27, 33, 86-87, 92, 119, 147-148
Digital Terrestrial Television (DTT), 87, 131
Digital Video Broadcasting (DVB), 156-157, 160, 169
Digital Video Broadcasting Cable (DVB-C), 150, 156-157, 169
Digital Video Compression, 4, 26-27, 161
Digital Video Disc (DVD), 28-29, 148
Digital Video Interconnection Types, 28, 162
Digital Video Service (DVS), 37

Digital Visual Interface (DVI), 28, 123, 125
Display Capability, 118, 120, 167
Distributed Workflow, 82, 165
Distribution Control, 70
Distribution Formats, 82, 165
Distribution Network, 7, 79, 84, 99, 101, 166
Distribution Rights, 54
DOCSIS 1.0, 149, 151, 168
DOCSIS 1.1, 149, 151, 169
DOCSIS 2.0, 149, 151, 169
DOCSIS 3.0, 150-151, 169
DOCSIS 3.1, 15, 34-35, 150-151, 169
Downloadable Conditional Access System (DCAS), 45
Dynamic Ad Insertion (DAI), 14, 161
Educational Access Channel, 64, 164
Electronic Program Guide (EPG), 56, 74, 138-142, 157, 168
Embedded Application, 126-127
Emergency Alert System (EAS), 64, 164
Enhanced Advertising, 13-14, 161
Enhanced Content, 49, 56, 163
European DOCSIS (EuroDOCSIS), 150, 169
Event Information Table (EIT), 158
Federal Communications Commission (FCC), 3, 11, 36, 44, 117, 143, 160
Fiber Ring, 99
Fiber Spur, 99
Fiber Type, 115, 167

www.ingramcontent.com/pod-product-compliance
Lightning Source LLC
Chambersburg PA
CBHW080547220326

41599CB00032B/6397